Test Bank to Accompany

Theatre
Fourth Edition

and

Theatre: Brief Version
Fourth Edition

by

Robert Cohen

Marilyn F. Moriarty
Hollins College

Mayfield Publishing Company
Mountain View, California
London • Toronto

International Standard Book Number: 1-55934-742-2

Manufactured in the United States of America

10 9 8 7 6 5 4 3 2 1

Mayfield Publishing Company
1280 Villa Street
Mountain View, California 94041

Preface

This printed test item file is offered in support of Robert Cohen's textbooks, *Theatre* and *Theatre: Brief Version,* both now in their fourth editions. This test bank includes approximately fifty multiple-choice questions per chapter with answers indicated by an asterisk. Additionally, five to seven essay questions are suggested for those of you fortunate enough to have smaller classes. For each test question, the page on which the topic is discussed in the book is indicated.

Test items are rarely universally admired, particularly if they have been drafted by another instructor. In this case we are blessed to have the assistance of Professor Marilyn F. Moriarty of Hollins College, who has crafted intelligent and thoughtful questions covering a range of difficulty. With this extensive test bank, even the most demanding instructor should find some assistance with quiz and examination preparation.

For this edition, the test banks for *Theatre* and *Theatre: Brief Version* have been combined. Chapter 7 in *Theatre: Brief Version* is a synthesis of Chapters 8 and 9 from *Theatre* and is the only chapter in the brief version not taken directly from *Theatre.* For this reason, the organization of this test bank is based on the order of chapters in *Theatre,* with Chapter 7 from the brief version appearing at the end. The following chart demonstrates the correspondence of chapters:

Theatre	Theatre: Brief Version
1. What Is the Theatre?	1. What Is the Theatre?
2. What Is a Play?	2. What Is a Play?
3. The Greeks	
4. The Middle Ages	
5. The Shakespearean Era	
6. Kabuki—and the Theatre of Asia	
7. The Royal Theatre	
8. The Modern Theatre: Realism	
9. The Modern Theatre: Antirealism	
10. Theatre Today	8. Theatre Today
11. The Actor	3. The Actor
12. The Playwright	4. The Playwright
13. Designers and Technicians	5. Designers and Technicians
14. The Director	6. The Director
15. The Critic	9. The Critic
	7. The Theatre of Our Times

How to Use This Test Bank: An Example

If you are testing on Chapter 3: The Actor, from *Theatre: Brief Version,* you will find the appropriate questions listed with Chapter 11 from *Theatre.* The page number listed immediately after the question indicates the page from *Theatre* on which the question is based. The page number labeled "Brief" is from *Theatre, Brief Version.*

Chapter 11/Brief: Chapter 3

The Actor

1. "Thespian" means
*   a. actor.
    b. the person in costume.
    c. falsifier.
    d. the person with a declamatory voice.
    360
    Brief: 62

Because carefully developed test banks are the exception rather than the rule in higher education theatre textbooks, we are very much interested in your suggestions for how this material might be improved. Please send any suggestions for additions or revisions that might be useful to you in your teaching to Theatre Editor, Mayfield Publishing Company, 1280 Villa Street, Mountain View, California 94041.

Chapter 1 / Brief: Chapter 1
What Is the Theatre?

 1. "Theatre" comes from *theatron,* which means
   a. acting place.
* b. seeing place.
   c. singing place.
   d. listening place.
   9
   Brief: 7

 2. "Drama" comes from the Greek *dran,* which means
   a. to make.
   b. to play.
* c. to do.
   d. to dance.
   9
   Brief: 7

3. "Theatre" signified all the following EXCEPT
   a. the building where the play is performed.
   b. the company of players.
* c. the stage and curtain.
   d. the professional acting activity.
   10
   Brief: 8

4. The minimal requirements for a theatre are
   a. a stage and an orchestra pit.
   b. a curtain and bleachers.
* c. a place to act and a place to watch.
   d. a director and a script.
   10
   Brief: 8

 5. The rigid distinction between the acting space and the audience space came to be formalized
   spatially when
* a. actors began to be paid.
   b. actors began to use make-up.
   c. acting became an unsavory, often illegal, profession.
   d. the audience gambled in their seats during the performance.
   11
   Brief: 9

6. The plays a theatre company produces are called its
   a. canon.
   b. script.
* c. repertory.
   d. text.
   12
   Brief: 10

7. In general, how much time goes into preparing a play for presentation?
* a. one year to produce
   b. two years to produce
   c. six years, including four years of writing
   d. six months
   14
   Brief: 12

8. Which theatrical craft fits the following description? Technicians execute in proper sequence and with carefully rehearsed timing the light and sound cues, the shifting of scenery, the placement and return of properties, and the assignment, laundering, and repair and change of costumes.
   a. stage managing
   b. producing
   c. directing
* d. running
   15
   Brief: 13

9. The task of securing all necessary personnel, space, and financing, supervising all production and promotion efforts, fielding all legal matters, and distributing the proceeds derived from receipts falls to the
   a. stage manager.
* b. producer.
   c. director.
   d. manager.
   15
   Brief: 13

10. The responsibilities for "running" a play, producing in all its complexity in performance and after performance, fall to the
    a. runners.
    b. builders.
    c. producer.
*   d. stage manager.
    15
    Brief: 13

11. When carpenters, costumers, wig-makers, electricians, make-up artists, recording and sound engineers, and painters translate the design into reality by constructing and finishing in detail the hardware of the show, they are engaged in
    a. house managing.
    b. producing.
    c. directing.
    * d. building.
    15
    Brief: 13

12. The responsibilities for admitting, seating, and providing for the general comfort of the audience fall to
    a. the director.
    b. the producer.
    * c. the house manager.
    d. the designer.
    15
    Brief: 13

13. The person who controls and develops the artistic product and provides it with a unified vision is
    a. the builder.
    * b. the director.
    c. the producer.
    d. the stage manager.
    15
    Brief: 13

14. Historically, theatres have grown up in close proximity with
    a. eating places.
    b. medicinal baths.
    * c. sports activities.
    d. political events.
    16
    Brief: 14

15. Which game offers an instance of the way that child's play prepares an individual for adult life, in this case by confronting the fear of separation from the parent?
    a. pin the tail on the donkey
    * b. hide-and-seek
    c. tag
    d. spin the bottle
    16
    Brief: 14

16. While both theatre and sport are public spectacles, theatre differs from sports activities because
   a. sports activities have more players.
 * b. ending is pre-ordained in theatre.
   c. theatre centers on a central protagonist.
   d. only sport involves conflict.
   16–17
   Brief: 14–15

 17. Which of the following is true of the art of theatre?
   a. Theatre is a pure art, in the hands of a single virtuoso writer.
   b. Up until the twentieth century, theatre had been the art of small groups of people.
 * c. Theatre is a collaborative art combining the arts of acting, writing, designing, and architecture.
   d. Theatre is an authoritarian art, dominated entirely by the director.
   17
   Brief: 15

 18. The distinctive feature of theatre that separates it from other arts is that theatre employs
   a. verse.
 * b. impersonation.
   c. scripts.
   d. symbolism.
   19
   Brief: 17

19. In classical times, what physical and symbolic element separated the actors from the audience?
   a. The actors spoke in verse.
 * b. The actors wore masks.
   c. The actors' names were printed in the program.
   d. The actors danced in special costumes.
   20
   Brief: 18

20. According to Denis Diderot, when the actor has perfected his or her art, it is the simulated character that seems to live before our eyes, while the real person has no apparent life at all. Diderot called this
 * a. the paradox of the actor.
   b. the metadramatic situation.
   c. existential frustration.
   d. psychological simulation.
   21
   Brief: 19

4

21. The first actor was
    a. Solon.
  * b. Thespis.
    c. Hippocrates.
    d. Aeschylus.
    22
    Brief: 20

22. The Greek word for actor was *hypokrites,* a word that originally meant
    a. dishonest.
  * b. answerer.
    c. feigner.
    d. speaker.
    22
    Brief: 20

23. The actor's impersonation of a character led to moral charges against the theatre, which maintained that actors were engaged in
    a. infidelity.
  * b. impiety.
    c. theft.
    d. treason.
    22
    Brief: 20

24. An action or series of actions taken for the ultimate benefit (attention, entertainment, enlightenment, or involvement) of someone else is called
    a. drama.
    b. theatre.
  * c. performance.
    d. tragedy.
    23
    Brief: 21

25. The mode of performance that continuously acknowledges the audience—as is the case of the nightclub performer who sings, dances, jokes, and asks for applause—is called
    a. the soliciting mode.
    b. the entertaining mode.
  * c. the direct mode.
    d. the indirect mode.
    24
    Brief: 22

26. The mode of performance during which the audience watches interactions that are staged as if no audience were present at all is called
   a. the direct mode.
 * b. the indirect mode.
   c. the feigned mode.
   d. the treacherous mode.
   24
   Brief: 22

27. The performance elicits the audience's participation by arousing in the audience the feeling of
 * a. pity.
   b. fear.
   c. joy.
   d. humor.
   24
   Brief: 22

28. Why did the playwright Bertolt Brecht use songs, signs, chalk talks, arguments, and slide projections in his productions?
   a. Brecht wanted to encourage active audience participation.
 * b. Brecht wanted to distance his audience.
   c. Brecht wanted to create a more realistic experience of life.
   d. Brecht wanted to create irony.
   25
   Brief: 23

29. The type of theatre that had as its goal the attempt to recreate life inside a room, and, thus, to preserve exact verisimilitude, or likeness to life, was called
   a. epic drama.
 * b. the theatre of the fourth wall removed.
   c. laboratory theatre.
   d. theatre of cruelty.
   26
   Brief: 24

30. What two things does an audience look for in a performance?
 * a. characters it can care about and actors it can admire
   b. good acoustics and a decorated set
   c. handsome actors and virtuous characters
   d. handsome actors and evil characters
   26
   Brief: 24

31. How does a theatrical performance differ from a video or filmed performance?
    a. The theatrical performance has a script, whereas video performances are most often impromptu.
    * b. The theatrical performance is live: the audience and performers share the same place and the same time and are aware of each other.
    c. Symbolism is far more important in theatrical performances than in video or film.
    d. Regional dialect is more effectively used in video than in theatre.
    27
    Brief: 25

32. All of the following are the advantages of live performance EXCEPT
    a. theatre provides a two-way communication between the audience and the actors and thus links them in an intrasocial bond.
    b. the audience experience of the play is collective and social by nature and thus unifies group responses.
    c. the immediacy of the drama makes every performance different and therefore both immediate and novel.
    * d. the playwright can hear his or her lines spoken the same way every night, and thus he can learn the range of each actor's voice.
    27–28
    Brief: 25–26

33. How does a theatrical performance differ from a happening or from performance art?
    a. Theatrical performances use impersonation.
    * b. Theatrical performances are scripted and rehearsed.
    c. Theatrical performances employ a decorated set and costumed performers.
    d. Theatrical performances involve the exchange of money, either to the actors or by the audience.
    29
    Brief: 27

34. Which of the following is true of the relationship between the playscript and the performance?
    * a. Virtually all important playscripts available to us today were published AFTER their initial performance.
    b. Virtually all important playscripts available to us today were published BEFORE their initial performance.
    c. Virtually all important playscripts available to us today omit the stage directions from the initial performance.
    d. Virtually all important playscripts available to us today include the appropriate facial gestures, expressions, and blocking.
    30
    Brief: 28

35. Which of the following is true of the relationship between the script and the play?
   a. The script is NOT the play.
   b. The script is EQUAL to the play.
   c. The script is not needed for the play.
   * d. More than one version of the script is needed for every play.
   30
   Brief: 28

36. The word "audience" comes from the Latin term that means
   a. those who watch.
   b. those who sit.
   * c. those who hear.
   d. those who sing.
   10
   Brief: 8

37. A collective group of theatre practitioners who have worked together in long-standing groups is called
   a. a gaggle.
   b. a collection.
   * c. a troupe.
   d. a posse.
   12
   Brief: 10

38. Which of the following is true of the difference between theatre and drama?
   a. Theatre is a subset of drama, so the difference is nugatory.
   b. Theatre uses *trompe l'oeil*, whereas drama uses *mise en abyme*.
   * c. "Theatre" refers to the process; "drama: refers to the product.
   d. Theatre emphasizes personae, whereas drama emphasizes plot.
   10
   Brief: 8

39. Which of all the theatrical crafts is usually executed away from the theatre building and its associated shops?
   a. running
   b. producing
   c. stage managing
   * d. playwriting
   15
   Brief: 13

40. Why is a theatrical performance sometimes called a "play"?
   * a. Not only is theatre like games and sports, it is also a simulation of adult activity.
   b. In theatre, there is always a clear winner and a clear loser.
   c. The plots of early plays were the object of gambling, especially in medieval Germany.
   d. Theatrical productions often preceded hunts and archery contests in classical Greece.
   16
   Brief: 14

41. What does the Nō drama in Japan have in common with early Greek drama?
   a. the use of stylized gestures and movements
   b. the text is sung or chanted
 * c. the use of the mask
   d. the use of painted scenery or screens to create a set
   20
   Brief: 18

42. The English word for person comes from the Latin word for
   a. humor.
   b. appearance.
 * c. mask.
   d. outfit.
   21
   Brief: 19

43. Which of the following is true of the twentieth-century use of the mask?
 * a. The mask has been supplanted by make-up, gestures, and character acting.
   b. The mask has been revitalized since Picasso discovered the African mask.
   c. The mask is now used only in folk drama.
   d. The mask is used only in religious drama.
   22
   Brief: 20

44. The twentieth-century emphasis on verisimilitude had which of the following consequences for acting?
   a. Character became less important and realistic sets became more important.
 * b. Character acting supplanted formal oratory.
   c. Only one actor at a time could be at the center of an emotionally charged scene.
   d. Violent scenes became the hallmark of good acting.
   22
   Brief: 20

45. Coleridge's term for the audience participation engendered by way of empathy was
 * a. willing suspension of disbelief.
   b. inscape.
   c. harmonic conversion.
   d. synergy.
   24
   Brief: 22

46. Which mode of performance does theatre employ?
 * a. indirect and direct
   b. direct
   c. indirect
   d. soliciting
   24
   Brief: 22

47. Theatrical performance differs from other kinds of performance because
    a. the audience is charged an admission fee.
*   b. theatre is live, scripted, and rehearsed.
    c. theatre alone employs dialect and scenery.
    d. theatre alone uses actors.
    26
    Brief: 24

48. Theatre is an art because
    a. it possesses form.
    b. it is not restricted by form.
*   c. it shapes the meaning of life.
    d. it has great imaginative scope.
    17
    Brief: 15

49. Which of the following is NOT an example of the shared history of theatre and sport?
    a. Roman circuses
    b. Elizabethan London theatres built to accommodate plays and bear-baiting
    c. the Greek competition for excellence, which was staged in the Dionysian festivals for theatre and the Olympian festivals for sports
*   d. the contemporary English fox hunt, which employs trumpet calls as entertainment for the riders
    16
    Brief: 14

ESSAY QUESTIONS

51. Define "impersonation," and explain the moral implications it holds for theatre. Why is impersonation the heart of theatre? How does the actor cope with the implied split in self? Incorporate Denis Diderot's remarks about the actor's paradox.

52. Agree or disagree: Theatre is not simply a collaborative art that requires the coordination of many *crafts;* it is also a collaborative experience because it requires an *audience.*

53. Take one of the crafts and explain the duties and responsibilities involved in it.

54. Explain the difference between a script and a performance.

55. Discuss the range of meanings contained in "theatre," and then explain how theatre differs from drama.

56. Explain why theatre is *work.*

Chapter 2 / Brief: Chapter 2
What Is a Play?

1. Why is a play considered art?
*   a.   It has a form that provides a frame for life.
     b.   It provides jocular entertainment.
     c.   It uses symbolism and scenery.
     d.   It embodies philosophical values.
     31–32
     Brief: 29–30

2. The final scene or scenes in a play devoted to tying up the loose ends after the climax are called
     a.   pathos.
     b.   *peripeteia.*
     c.   *anagnorisis.*
*   d.   denouement.
     59
     Brief: 57

3. Aristotle's term for the character's recognition of some fundamental truth or of some reversal is
     a.   *peripeteia.*
*   b.   *anagnorisis.*
     c.   pathos.
     d.   *catharsis.*
     58
     Brief: 56

4. "Genre" means
     a.   category or kind.
     b.   origin or birth.
     c.   a play that can be performed.
     d.   a form of irony.
     34
     Brief: 32

5. The point of highest tension in a play, when the conflicts of the play are at their fullest expression, is called
     a.   empathy.
*   b.   climax.
     c.   crescendo.
     d.   denouement.
     58
     Brief: 56

6. Which of the following is true of the different origins of tragedy and comedy?
   a. Tragedy was an outgrowth of certain prehistoric religious rituals, whereas comedy was a secular entertainment developed out of bawdy skits and popular revels.
   b. Tragedy grew out of the celebration of a warrior's death in battle, whereas comedy emerged from the point of view of the common people around the hero.
   c. Tragedy emerged from an attempt to illustrate Greek myths of rebirth and renewal, whereas comedy arose from the illustration of pastoral poetry and songs.
   d. Tragedy arose from the dialogue as a form of philosophical inquiry, and comedies arose from parodies of tragic plays.
   34
   Brief: 32

7. The central character in any type of drama is called
   a. the tragic hero.
   * b. the protagonist.
   c. the *agon.*
   d. the antagonist.
   35
   Brief: 33

8. In Greek tragedy, the central character
   a. undergoes a decline in fortune leading to suffering and death.
   b. fails to understand his or her fortune.
   c. is always descended from the gods.
   d. always has the option of avoiding conflicts.
   35–36
   Brief: 33–34

9. In a Greek play, the lead character, who carries the action, is opposed by a figure called
   a. the senex.
   b. the contagonist.
   * c. the antagonist.
   d. the protagonist.
   36
   Brief: 34

10. The purging or cleansing of pity and terror that the audience develops during the climax of a tragedy is called
    a. *hamartia.*
    b. *kothurnoi.*
    c. *anagnorisis.*
    * d. *catharsis.*
    36
    Brief: 34

11. Tragic suffering differs from pathetic or sad feelings in that
    a.   the cause of tragic suffering is narrated rather than dramatized.
    b.   pathetic feelings originate in the character's denial of his or her fate.
*   c.   the tragic hero takes on a larger-than-life dimension because of his or her struggle against superhuman antagonists.
    d.   the pathetic hero's greatest virtue is humility rather than courage.
    36
    Brief: 34

12. According to Aristotle, which of the following was the model of a great tragedy?
    a.   the anonymous *Epic of Gilgamesh*
    b.   Euripides' *The Trojan Women*
*   c.   Sophocles' *Oedipus Tyrannos*
    d.   Aeschylus' *Oresteia*
    36
    Brief: 34

 13. Which modern play challenges Aristotle's definition of tragedy by having the lead character come from the lower classes?
    a.   Eugene O'Neill's *The Hairy Ape*
*   b.   Arthur Miller's *Death of a Salesman*
    c.   Tennessee Williams's *Cat on a Hot Tin Roof*
    d.   Henrik Ibsen's *Hedda Gabler*
    36
    Brief: 34

 14. The first author of written comedies known to us from the Greek world is
    a.   Sophocles.
    b.   Aeschylus.
*   c.   Aristophanes.
    d.   Eumenides.
    36
    Brief: 34

 15. How does tragedy differ from comedy?
    a.   They differ thematically: tragedy deals with serious human conflict; comedy deals with trivial events.
*   b.   They differ structurally: tragic plots end in suffering; comic plots have a happy ending.
    c.   The audience response is different: tragedy elicits catharsis; comedy elicits laughter.
    d.   The meter of the language differs: tragedy is written in blank verse; comedy is written in prose.
    37
    Brief: 35

16. How do tragic and comic characterizations differ?
    * a. Comic characters are individuals whose problems are social rather than cosmic.
      b. Comic characters are generally drawn larger-than-life and confuse cosmic problems with superstition.
      c. Tragic characters are motivated by ambition rather than by psychological problems, whereas comic characters are motivated by problems with etiquette.
      d. Tragic characters rely upon dialogue to reveal their intentions, whereas comic characters rely upon soliloquy to reveal their intentions.
      37
      Brief: 35

17. According to Horace, comedy should offer *utile dulce,* or
      a. practical wisdom.
      b. useful insight.
    * c. sweet instruction.
      d. futile entertainment.
      38
      Brief: 36

18. Which of the following is NOT a modern author of dramatic comedy?
      a. George Bernard Shaw
      b. Simon Gray
      c. George Kaufman
    * d. Samuel Johnson
      38
      Brief: 36

19. What genres did the Middle Ages contribute to the canon of dramatic writing?
      a. tragicomedies and satires
    * b. interludes and cycle plays
      c. pastoral comedy
      d. the verse play in three acts
      38
      Brief: 36

20. Which genre did Shakespeare create?
      a. the tragicomedy
    * b. the history play
      c. the pastoral satire
      d. the play-within-the-play
      38
      Brief: 36

21. This type of drama, exemplified by Plautus's *Amphitryon,* bridges genres: it maintains a serious theme although the tone varies from grave to humorous; it concludes without a violent catharsis.
    a. historical romance
    * b. tragicomedy
    c. dark comedy
    d. satire
    39
    Brief: 37

22. A play that dramatizes the key events in the life of a king or head of state, such as Shakespeare's *Henry IV,* is called
    * a. a history play.
    b. a tragicomedy.
    c. a dark comedy.
    d. a burlesque.
    38
    Brief: 36

23. This kind of play begins comically but ends disturbingly, leaving the audience with the impression of an unresolved universe surrounding the play's characters.
    a. history play
    b. tragicomedy
    * c. dark comedy
    d. burlesque
    39
    Brief: 37

24. The most significant difference between tragicomedy and dark comedy is
    a. the ending: tragicomedies end happily; dark comedies end sadly.
    b. the ending: tragicomedies end sadly; dark comedies end happily.
    c. the characters: tragicomic characters are riddled with doubt; dark comic characters are riddled with guilt.
    d. the characters: tragicomic characters are undone by sex; dark comic characters are undone by greed.
    39
    Brief: 37

25. Which of the following is NOT an instance of a dark comedy?
    a. Shakespeare's *The Tempest*
    b. George Bernard Shaw's *Major Barbara*
    c. Samuel Beckett's *All That Fall*
    * d. Arthur Koestler's *Darkness at Noon*
    39
    Brief: 37

26. Plays that purport to be serious but that are in fact often trivial entertainment embellished with spectacular staging, sententious dialogue, and highly suspenseful—and contrived—plotting are called
a. dark comedy.
b. tragicomedy.
* c. melodrama.
d. farce.
39
Brief: 37

27. A wild, hilarious treatment of a trivial theme, usually based on a stock theme such as identical twins, switched identities, lovers in closets, full-stage chases, misheard instructions, various disrobings, and discoveries and disappearances, characterizes this kind of genre.
a. dark comedy
b. melodrama
* c. farce
d. tragicomedy
40–41
Brief: 38–39

28. This genre, of fairly recent development, relies upon authentic evidence used as the basis for portraying relatively recent historical events.
a. musical
b. melodrama
c. tragicomedy
* d. documentary
41
Brief: 39

29. This genre is identified by its extensive musical score—particularly its vocal score—and has been considered America's greatest contribution to the theatre.
a. soap opera
b. music video
c. burlesque
* d. musical
42
Brief: 40

30. Which critical work analyzed a play through its division into parts?
* a. *Poetics*
b. *The Republic*
c. *Ars Moriendi*
d. *Ars Amatoria*
43
Brief: 41

16

31. The components of a play that Aristotle lists, in order of importance, are
   a. script, stage, actor, playwright, and government support.
 * b. plot, character, theme, diction, music, and spectacle.
   c. irony, pastoral, idyll, satire, and humor.
   d. reversal, tragic flaw, recognition, catharsis, and subplots.
   43
   Brief: 41

32. What is the difference between plot and story?
   a. The terms are synonymous.
 * b. "Plot" refers to the structure of events; "story" refers to a narrative that contains a plot.
   c. A plot has a moral, whereas a story has suspense.
   d. A plot can be turned into a play, but only a story can be turned into prose fiction.
   43–44
   Brief: 41–42

33. The two primary demands of plot are
   a. recognition and irony.
 * b. suspense and logic.
   c. suspense and discovery.
   d. logic and a conclusion.
   44
   Brief: 42

34. In general, a character is
   a. an exaggerated personality type.
   b. the person who wears the mask.
 * c. a "person" in a play as performed by an actor.
   d. anyone who speaks from a stage.
   44
   Brief: 42

35. Aristotle's term for the play's overall statement, its topic, central idea, or message, is
   a. onomatopoeia.
   b. thesis.
 * c. theme.
   d. pathos.
   45
   Brief: 43

36. This element of drama refers not only to the pronunciation of spoken dialogue but also to the literary nature of the play's text, including its tone, imagery, articulation, and use of such literary forms as verse, rhyme, metaphor, jest, apostrophe, and epigram.
   a. episodic discourse
   b. theme
 * c. diction
   d. alliteration
   46
   Brief: 44

37. This element describes the play's use of rhythm and sounds, either by way of music or by way of the orchestration of such noises as muffled drumbeats, gunshots, and animal cries.
    a. diction
    b. syllabic counterpoint
  * c. music
    d. orchestra
    46, 48
    Brief: 44, 46

38. The visual aspect of the play, including the scenery, costumes, lighting, make-up, and the overall look of the stage, is accommodated by the element of theatre known as
    a. allusion.
    b. intermezzo.
    c. cortina magica.
  * d. spectacle.
    48–49
    Brief: 46–47

39. The agreement between the audience and the actor, which includes a whole set of tacit understandings that form the context of playwatching, is called
    a. spectacle.
  * b. convention.
    c. theme.
    d. ars poetica.
    49
    Brief: 47

40. When one actor turns directly away from the others and speaks to the audience, the other characters are presumed not to hear him. This is the convention of
    a. the proscenium.
    b. the cyclorama.
  * c. the aside.
    d. the missing fourth wall.
    49
    Brief: 47

41. Dramatic conventions
    a. are universal, the same for all plays at all times.
    b. vary with place but not time.
    c. vary with time but not place.
  * d. vary with time and place.
    50
    Brief: 48

42. According to Aristotle, how should every play be structured?
    a. Every play should have a beginning, middle, and end.
    b. Every play should have a prologue at the beginning to provide exposition and an epilogue at the end to explain the denouement.
    c. Every play should start with the beginning of the character's existence and not with the beginning of the action.
    d. Every play should begin with a soliloquy that is questioned by the chorus.
    51
    Brief: 49

43. Events of the drama that surround the performance of the play, such as the publicity, admission, and seating, are called
    a. metatheatrical.
    * b. paratheatrical.
    c. hypotheatrical.
    d. cryptotheatrical.
    51
    Brief: 49

44. One of the oldest ways of publicizing a theatrical performance is by means of
    a. commissioned painters who create frescos in public plazas.
    b. staging the opening night on national holidays.
    c. an actor or mime who performs excerpts in public places.
    * d. a procession.
    51
    Brief: 49

45. In ancient Greece, the name given to a conclave of playwrights and actors who were introduced in a large public meeting and given a chance to speak about the plays they were to present was
    a. *agon.*
    b. *agora.*
    * c. *proagon.*
    d. *anteus.*
    51
    Brief: 49

46. "Box-office revenue" refers to
    a. the fees charged the audience for admission to the performance in addition to the contributions made by patrons.
    b. the contribution of patrons and the government support.
    * c. the fees charged the audience for admission to the performance.
    d. the government contribution by way of money, services, or space.
    52
    Brief: 50

47. Background information that the audience must possess in order to understand the happenings in the action of the play and that is presented within the play is called
    a.   recognition.
*   b.   exposition.
    c.   denouement.
    d.   paraphrase.
    53
    Brief: 51

48. Which of the following offers a way for the playwright to supply exposition?
    a.   the program notes that an audience must read before it sees the play
*   b.   a prologue directly providing information through a speech
    c.   a talk show during which the actor relays information to the viewing audience
    d.   posters or playbills that tell the audience what will happen in the play
    55
    Brief: 53

49. In play construction, the single action that initiates the major conflict of the play is called
    a.   exposition.
*   b.   inciting incident.
    c.   characterization.
    d.   denouement.
    58
    Brief: 56

50. The Greek word for passion (and which includes suffering) that refers to the depth of feeling evoked by tragedy is
    a.   *ethos.*
    b.   *bathos.*
*   c.   *pathos.*
    d.   *kommos.*
    58
    Brief: 56

ESSAY QUESTIONS

51. Apply Aristotle's elements of drama to Aeschylus' play *Prometheus Bound.*

52. Define "conventions" and explain how you see those conventions working in a play of your choice.

53. Discuss pre-play activities in terms of the conventions of the drama.

54. According to Aristotle, plot is the soul of drama. Discuss the way that the other elements of the drama support the plot.

55. The curtain call functions as an important convention in the drama. Explain its importance, especially in terms of the actor's paradox, the economical relationship between audience and actors.

Chapter 3

The Greeks

1. When theatre historians speak of the "Greek theatre" they are referring to
* a. Athens in the fifth century.
   b. Athens and Sparta from fourth to the third century A.D.
   c. the collected body of Greek drama from the fifth century B.C. to the birth of Christ.
   d. all classical (Greek, Roman, and neoclassical) drama.
   65

2. Which of the following is NOT a famous Greek playwright?
   a. Sophocles
   b. Euripides
* c. Pericles
   d. Aeschylus
   65

3. Which of the following is NOT an extant classical text?
   a. forty-three intact plays
   b. Aristotle's *Poetics*
   c. numerous anecdotes and commentaries about the plays
* d. Tantalus' book on scene painting
   66

4. Which of the following characterizes actual classical Greek drama?
* a. Greek drama was vivid, spectacular, bawdy, blasphemous, and passionate.
   b. Greek drama was restrained, stately, dignified, and noble.
   c. Greek drama was intellectual, a theatre of ideas only, focusing on the mind rather than the body, with characters that represented general human abstractions like "The Good," "The True," and "The Beautiful."
   d. Greek drama was physical, bloodily spectacular, and melodramatic and emphasized spectacles that showed the actors' acrobatic prowess.
   66

5. Which emotion or attitude underlay all ritual in Greek religion?
   a. love of the gods
   b. love of human beings
* c. dread of the gods
   d. fear of human violence
   66

6. The god of fertility, wine, agriculture, and sexuality was
   a. Apollo.
   b. Athena.
   c. Mercury.
* d. Dionysus.
   66

21

7. In classical Greek plays, this ensemble of characters represents the general public view of the play.
   a. *parodos*
   b. *choregus*
 * c. chorus
   d. *kothurnoi*
   82, 86

8. A shaman is
 * a. a religious leader who is credited with an understanding of the superhuman and who has the authority to reveal it to the masses.
   b. a writer of poetry who is so gifted that he is credited with divine inspiration.
   c. a medical practitioner with specialized knowledge of herbs, grasses, and poisons.
   d. a philosopher with a special interest in the culture of other countries.
   67

9. The *dithyrambos* was
   a. an austere religious sacrifice involving burning incense and consecrating a bull to Apollo.
   b. a combination song and dance routine performed on the spring equinox and celebrated with flowers, grasses, and the blessing of ships.
 * c. an ancient, drunken dance-chant fertility ritual that celebrated the birth of the wine god.
   d. a rite of passage symbolizing the transition from virginity to marriage, sanctified by the reading of oracles from Delphi and blessed with water from the Kastalian spring.
   67

10. Greek dramatists wrote plays in tetralogies, groups of four plays composed of
    a. a comedy, a tragedy, a tragicomedy that linked the themes, and a burlesque.
 * b. three tragedies and one satyr play.
    c. two comedies and two tragedies.
    d. a short operetta, two comedies, and a tragedy.
    69

11. A satyr play was
    a. a play that featured a sprite, a satyr, or a wood nymph as its central character.
 * b. a short bawdy farce that parodied the events of tragedy.
    c. a play located in a woodland setting, where satyrs were believed to live.
    d. any play with at least one character who was a composite being of any type, whether satyr, centaur, or mermaid.
    69

12. Of all the collected plays that have come down to us, only this assemblage remains intact.
    a. Homer's *Iliad* and *Odyssey*
 * b. Aeschylus' tetralogy, *The Oresteia*
    c. Euripides' comic and tragic treatment of the Trojan War
    d. Aristotle's *Poetics*
    70

13. Which of the following genres most closely preserved the spirit of the dithyramb?
    a. tragedy
    b. tragicomedy
    c. pastoral elegy
* d. satyr play
    70

14. The Greek word for tragedy was *tragoidia,* which means
    a. sad death.
    b. great hero.
* c. goat song.
    d. song of woe.
    71

15. The central difference between the satyr play/tragedy and the dithyramb was that
    a. the dithyramb maintained a religious tone, whereas the tone of the tragedy/satyr play was secular.
* b. the tragedy/satyr play added an actor to the performance.
    c. the dithyramb was always performed by women, whereas only men were permitted to perform in a tragedy or satyr play.
    d. the dithyramb was always keyed to special dates on the astronomical and religious calendar, whereas the tragedy/satyr play could be performed at any time of the year.
    71

16. The first word for actor was
* a. *hypokrites,* meaning "answerer."
    b. *catharsis,* meaning "imposter."
    c. *peripeteia,* meaning "false identity."
    d. *spargasmos,* meaning "impersonator."
    71

17. Which contribution to the drama did Thespis NOT make?
    a. the invention of the mask
    b. the adoption of impersonation
* c. scene painting
    d. dialogue
    71

18. Which of the following is NOT true about the use of actors on the stage?
    a. Aeschylus increased the number of actors on stage to two.
    b. Sophocles added a third actor to enable "overheard" dialogue situations.
    c. Sophocles increased the dithyrambic chorus to fifteen.
* d. Aeschylus added the figure of the woman.
    71

19. What image of God does Aeschylus give us in *Prometheus Bound?*
    a. Zeus, while fundamentally fond of humans, displays a personal vendetta toward Prometheus.
    b. Zeus is benevolent toward humans and Prometheus.
  * c. Zeus is inimical not only to Prometheus but also to humankind.
    d. Zeus, possessing foreknowledge, binds Prometheus to the rock for his own good and for the greater common good of humanity.
    80

20. Even though he is bound to a rock, Prometheus displays his own power through
    a. a massive physical strength that transcends the natural bonds on him.
  * b. the emotional power of poetry to move its auditors.
    c. his patient capacity to endure all manner of suffering.
    d. his rapier wit and intellect that employs logic to convince his auditors of his rightness.
    81

21. Which of the following is NOT true of the Greek chorus?
  * a. The chorus suppressed the individual's ability to voice private opinions.
    b. The chorus stood metaphorically and literally between the principal characters and the audience.
    c. The chorus enabled the playwright to bridge narrative and dramatic forms.
    d. The chorus permitted the insertion of internal monologues as well as incendiary public addresses.
    82

22. Which of the following most accurately describes the central tension in *Prometheus Bound?*
    a. The contrast between Prometheus' will to freedom and the chains that bind him shows the intransigence of the individual and the need to obey and conform to the will of the Father, Zeus.
  * b. The contrast between Prometheus' will to freedom and the chains that pin him to the rock symbolizes rebellious humanity straining against the shackles of oppressive authority.
    c. The contrast between Prometheus' isolation on the mountain top and the visitors who come to speak with him symbolizes the need for the all-powerful to sustain social relations.
    d. The contrast between Prometheus' isolation on the mountain top and the visitors who come to speak with him shows the importance of courtesy in social situations.
    82–83

23. Today the term "Promethean" is used to describe
    a. a character whose physical strength far outweighs his intellectual or emotional capacity.
    b. a character like the fool or clown who retains a sense of humor in the face of the most oppressive circumstances.
  * c. a character whose actions, by their extreme courage and recklessness, seem to redefine human possibility.
    d. a character whose actions seem foolhardy and reckless and who thereby receives the punishment he deserves.
    83

24. The theme of *Prometheus Bound* is that of
 * a. probing deeply into the theme of freedom of thought.
   b. the need to show humility before all fathers.
   c. the capacity of love to rectify all situations.
   d. the danger of letting a double take over one's identity.
   87

25. Which of the following incorrectly pairs the playwright with the play?
   a. Sophocles: *Oedipus Tyrannos*
 * b. Aeschylus: *Prometheus Unbound*
   c. Euripides: *The Trojan Women*
   d. Shelley: *Prometheus Unbound*
   87, 95

26. The device by which the playwright offers revelations about past events in the play or characters' lives is called
   a. denouement.
   b. crisis.
   c. prophecy.
 * d. exposition.
   88

27. The device used to offer revelations about the future is called
 * a. prophecy.
   b. irony.
   c. metaphor.
   d. onomatopoeia.
   88

28. "Dramatic irony" is a term that describes
   a. the reversal in a character's fate from bad to good.
 * b. a theatrical contrivance that enables the audience to understand the characters' situation better than the characters do.
   c. a soliloquy when overheard by other characters.
   d. the clash in color used to separate characters with different points of view.
   90

29. Because he was so adept at the use of dramatic irony, which playwright is credited with "inventing" it?
   a. Aristophanes
   b. Euripides
 * c. Sophocles
   d. Aeschylus
   90

30. *Hamartia* refers to
    * a. the flaw, error, or frailty in a great hero.
    b. a plot device introduced to bring resolution through artificial means.
    c. a shift in stage lighting to allow characters onstage to change the decor.
    d. a character's reversal in fortunes.
    93

31. *Anagnorisis* refers to
    a. the audience's response to tragedy.
    b. the physical configuration of the stage.
    * c. the central character's recognition of a higher truth.
    d. the will of the gods.
    93

32. Which of the following events does NOT offer the opportunity for catharsis?
    a. a bull fight
    b. psychotherapy
    * c. religious meditation
    d. tragic drama
    93–94

33. Sigmund Freud described the Oedipus complex in this way:
    * a. the Oedipus myth springs from the universal desire of the male child to unite sexually with his mother and from his corollary desire to murder his father.
    b. the Oedipus myth springs from the universal desire of the male child to completely control his past and surrounding events by summoning all persons around him to answer his questions.
    c. the Oedipus complex springs from the scientific impulse to control contagion or disease.
    d. The Oedipus myth dramatizes the need each individual has to confront mythological authority, like the sphinx, in order to conquer it through wit.
    94

34. The existential view of *Oedipus* maintains that
    a. Oedipus encounters the "other" in the figure of the sphinx.
    * b. the play shows a quest for identity in universe that confirms neither (quest or identity) and repudiates both.
    c. the play shows the need for the individual to continue a search although all others counsel him against it.
    d. Oedipus acts out of repression when he attempts to avoid his destiny.
    95

35. What historical event might have inspired Euripides' writing of *The Trojan Women?*
    a. the slaughter of children in Athens when vultures grew hungry
    * b. the Athenian slaughter of and conquest of the innocent Melians
    c. the arrival of the barbarian tribes at the gate of Athens
    d. the death of Socrates and the grief it brought to his wife, Xanthippe
    95

36. Most Roman plays
    a. dealt with Roman themes and involved stories of noble families.
    * b. dealt with Greek themes, in Greek costumes, acting out Greek legends.
    c. dealt with every type of story relating to the founding of a dynasty although the plays were performed in Latin.
    d. dealt with religious themes and were combined with ritual ceremonies.
    96

37. Roman plays differed from Greek plays in that
    * a. Roman plays were relatively free of cultural ritual, religious odes, serious politics, and Dionysian revelry.
    b. Roman plays, composed of three acts rather than five, required less time to perform.
    c. Roman plays integrated the sacrifice of a live animal in the pre-play activities, whereas Greek plays did not.
    d. Roman plays always treated the life of a king or caesar as if he were a god, whereas Greek plays presented the gods as independent characters.
    96

38. *Persona* is Latin for
    a. personality.
    * b. mask or character represented by the mask.
    c. humor—as in melancholy, sanguine, bilious, phlegmatic.
    d. temperament expressed in terms of temperature, as in *hot*-blooded.
    96

39. Which of the following is true of Titus Maccius Plautus (c. 254–184 B.C.)?
    * a. His twenty-one plays are fast-paced, joke-filled, lusty stage romps filled with songs.
    b. His twenty-one plays chronicle the founding and glory of Rome through noble and elevated language spoken by Senators.
    c. His twenty-one plays show his marriage of the existential themes of Greek tragedy with the light-hearted ambiance of the pastoral idyll.
    d. His twenty-one plays, dealing with religious themes, were prohibited from performance owing to the Roman emperor's claim to be both king and god.
    96

40. One of Plautus's characters, *Miles Gloriosus,* has become what type of character?
    a. the evil twin in plots of mistaken identity
    b. the prototype of the misanthrope, who hates all mankind
    * c. the braggart soldier
    d. the long-suffering and faithful husband duped by his wife, his servants, his customers, and his friends
    96

41. Which of the following is true of Publius Terentius Afer (c. 190–159 B.C.)?
    a. Though he was born from the merchant class and had a promising career as a silvermaker, his plays, written as an avocation, were prized for their joviality and slapstick.
    * b. This freed African slave wrote six comedies, based on Greek models, that were highly prized during the Middle Ages for their rhetorical excellence and philosophic depth.
    c. Terence was the pen name of a female writer who was married to a Senator and who enjoyed a career as a social entertainer, the world of which she lampooned in sixteen social satires compared only to those of Juvenal in their bite.
    d. This tutor of Nero wrote tragedies adapted from the Greek but was eventually poisoned by Nero for his representation of the emperor as slavish.
    97

42. Senecan drama was characterized by
    a. its serene and elevated language, well-constructed plot, and expansive use of stage machines like the pulley to represent the intervention of the gods.
    b. its suspense and mystery plot combined with a surprise and often revolutionary ending.
    * c. its horrific power in gruesome, highly charged scenes of passion and violence.
    d. the use of women dancers, lightly costumed in veils, and Seneca's practice of releasing doves and dropping flower petals on the stage at the close of his comedies.
    97

43. A playing space in Greek theatre, used primarily by the chorus, the circular ground-level acting area in front of the stagehouse was called
    a. *skene.*
    * b. *orchestra.*
    c. *thymele.*
    d. *theatron.*
    72

44. The Greek version of a dressing room was a wooden changing room called
    * a. *skene.*
    b. *orchestra.*
    c. *thymele.*
    d. *theatron.*
    72

45. The actors' footwear, which exaggerated his height on the stage, was called
    * a. *kothurnoi.*
    b. *onkoi.*
    c. *chiton.*
    d. *himation.*
    74

46. A "coming-forward" of a character in Old Greek comedy who then gives a direct address to the audience in the middle of the play is called
 *   a.   *parabasis.*
    b.   paradox.
    c.   *parodos.*
    d.   *paratheatron.*
    77

47. A "going-in" song or ode sung in the passage for entrances (one of two passageways between the stage house and audience area), employed primarily for the entrance and exit of the chorus, was called
    a.   *parabasis.*
    b.   paradox.
 *   c.   *parodos.*
    d.   *paratheatron.*
    77

48. What term, the root word of "agony," refers to the major struggles and interaction in Greek tragedy?
    a.   protagonist
    b.   antagonist
    c.   *proagon*
 *   d.   *agon*
    77

49. Dithyrambs were
 *   a.   literary songs and dances.
    b.   verse satires accompanied by pipes.
    c.   elegiac verses lamenting the death of a shepherd.
    d.   poems that presented an ideal vision of a society in which everyone was equal.
    68

50. In the context of Greek theatrical history, orgies were
    a.   large parties that occasioned a special drama.
    b.   wild free-for-alls involving sex and drugs.
 *   c.   tribal festivals, four times a year, during which *dithyrambos* were performed.
    d.   parties celebrating the local tyrant's name day.
    68

51. Which emotion lies at the roots of classical drama?
    a.   anxiety
    b.   temperance
    c.   fear
 *   d.   ecstasy
    68

52. What influence contributed to the "domestication" of the dithyramb?
  * a. Foreign trade brought about the need for a more secular and civilized entertainment than the spring ecstatic ritual allowed.
    b. Auguries and omens received from priests warned the citizens that a plague would follow unless the drama were made more secular.
    c. The Peloponnesian War, which sapped Athens and Sparta of their economic sources, depleted the spirit of life that stood behind the dithyramb.
    d. As the city government of Athens grew politically more democratic, public taste came to reflect the greatest aesthetic common denominator.

    68–69

53. According to the nineteenth-century German philosopher Friedrich Nietzsche, Greek drama could be understood as a synthesis between
    a. the pastoral life of shepherds and the more urbane wit of the city dwellers.
  * b. Dionysian ecstasy and Apollonian rationality.
    c. the spirit of war loosed by the Peloponnesian War and the spirit of love exemplified by Venus.
    d. the sensibility of the ruling class and that of the merchant class.

    69

ESSAY QUESTIONS

54. What is the function of the grotesque or the fantastic in Aeschylus's *Prometheus Bound?* In this play we see a chorus of women who leave so quickly, they forget to put on their shoes. They arrive in hovering vehicles, and Oceanus arrives on a four-legged bird. Io, in her bovine affliction, tells a story as grotesque as it is cruel. Does the fantastic/grotesque reflect the condition of the world? Is Prometheus (and/or Zeus) an extension of the grotesque, or does he offer an antidote to it?

55. Compare and contrast the ways the gods are represented in two Greek plays.

    Many Greek plays rely in some way on a representation of the gods, but the gods appear in different forms: through language (threat or prophecy); through intermediaries (servants or seers); or in human form. Consider not only the *role* of the gods within the plot but also the *manner* in which they are presented.

    Try to make some kind of point through your comparison. How does the manner in which the gods appear reflect the general tone of the play itself? Do the gods appear more powerful when we see them in human form, or does the human form reveal their human weakness? Do the plays subvert or support the authority of the gods?

56. Take a Greek tragedy, and explain how the tragic individual relates to the human community. Does an individual's encounter with the universe lead him or her to become separated from the human community or to return to that community for strength?

57. Explain the growth of the Greek drama in terms of the progressive increase in numbers of persons on the stage. What implications might this physical change have for the dramaturgy?

Chapter 4

The Middle Ages

1. "The Middle Ages" describes the period of history
   a. between the sack of Constantinople and the building of Chartres cathedral.
   b. between the death of Saladin and the birth of William Shakespeare.
* c. between the fall of Rome and the coming of the Renaissance.
   d. between the First Crusade and the invention of the printing press.
   101

2. Which of the following is NOT true of the Middle Ages?
   a. The Middle Ages were dominated by a feudal political and economic system.
   b. The Middle Ages were dominated by a chivalric order of knights and a sharp differentiation between nobility and peasants.
   c. The physical and social technology lacked the sophistication of either the Roman era or the Renaissance.
* d. The literature of the Middle Ages, written in French, celebrated national achievements.
   101

3. The High Middle Ages extended from
* a. the tenth and eleventh centuries onward.
   b. the ninth through the twelfth centuries.
   c. 1299 to 1350.
   d. the twelfth through the fourteenth centuries.
   101–102

4. Which of the following did medieval drama NOT share with Greek theatre?
   a. Both theatres ritualized the resurrection of a divine figure.
   b. Both theatres were public and communal, attracting a mass audience for the celebration of a common *mythos*.
   c. Both theatres were functioning parts of an evolving civic government.
* d. Both theatres produced playwrights of great talent and magnificence and with social and mystical status.
   102

5. A trope is
   a. the name for a short skit.
* b. a series of liturgical elaborations that expanded the services of the Mass.
   c. a verse poem sung in church.
   d. a two-act play that ends happily.
   102

6. The liturgical trope *Quem Queritas*
* a. celebrates the visit of the three Marys to the tomb of the crucified Christ.
   b. celebrates the baptism of John the Baptist.
   c. enacts the birth of Christ and a visitation by angels.
   d. enacts the visitation of the three Magi to Christ on the feast of the Epiphany.
   102

31

7. Which dramatic element was NOT present in the *Quem Queritas* trope?
   a. dialogue
 * b. impersonation
   c. use of props
   d. music and song
   102

8. From which text do we receive instructions for the enactment of *Quem Queritas?*
   a. the *Miserare* of Regina of Milan in 675 A.D.
   b. the *Catalogue of Christian Practices* by Augustine of Hippo in 1012
   c. a note written by an architect on plans for a church in Wales in 977
 * d. the *Concordia Regularis,* prepared in 980 by St. Ethelwold, bishop of Winchester
   102–103

9. The function of the *Quem Queritas* trope was
   a. to stand in as a lesson in theology by explaining the mystery of the faith.
 * b. to ritualize and bring to life the most important moment in the story of Christ.
   c. to entertain through means of religious instruction.
   d. to show that Christian mysteries were joyous by bringing humor to ritual.
   103

10. "Vulgar language" refers to
 * a. the common language of the people—French, German, Flemish, English—as opposed to Latin, which was the universal language of the day.
   b. the idiolect of peasants rather than the more elevated language of merchants.
   c. words referring to specific parts of the body, normally referred to by pointing.
   d. words applied to animals, furniture, or any inanimate object.
   104

11. What factors contributed to Pope Innocent II's decree in 1240 that drama could no longer be played in church?
   a. Priests were growing too popular as actors, and the audience began to mix up the priestly office with the characters priests impersonated.
   b. The clergy had begun to collect lavish robes and other riches from patrons seeking religious dispensations.
 * c. The drama had grown too large for presentation in cathedrals, and Church officers rebelled against the growing secular authority of the plays.
   d. The church-going audience grew too lax in church and brought their food, wine, and other amenities to make themselves more comfortable during the performance.
   104

12. Which of the following was NOT an effect of a theatre devoted to the glorification of Christ?
   a. The theatre formed a powerful force for moral instruction of an illiterate but ethically receptive audience.
 * b. The theatre supported farming and other agrarian pursuits by its need for oxen and horses to draw the pageant wagons.
   c. The theatre facilitated the urbanization of a rural society.
   d. The theatre offered festive amusement and entertainment after a long winter locked in against the cold.
   104

13. Which of the following is NOT an example of a typically medieval kind of play?
    a. pageant plays
    b. cycle plays
    c. miracle plays
  * d. history plays
    105

14. Mystery plays and miracle plays shared the same patterns EXCEPT which of the following?
    a. a series of playlets inspired by stories from the Bible
    b. a common language, which was that of the populace
    c. the plays were consistently presented in sequence, performed in, on, or around a stage or series of stages
  * d. each town shared the same handwritten script, which was handed from father to son over the generations
    105

15. A *mansion* was
    a. an elaborately constructed house.
  * b. a temporarily crafted stage that was set up in a public square and then moved about from day to day.
    c. the box that appears onstage to be a part of the scenery but that actually holds all the props needed for the play.
    d. the platform segment which bore the stage planks.
    105

16. Corpus Christi plays were so called because
  * a. they were commonly performed during the church festival of Corpus Christi sometime between late May and late June.
    b. the theme of the play always involved a celebration of the body of Christ in all its forms.
    c. they were named after the author, Desiderius Corpus.
    d. before the play began, a priest celebrated the Mass, a central feature of which was the transubstantiation or symbolic creation of Christ's body.
    106

17. Of the forty-eight York Corpus Christi plays,
  * a. individual playlets were allocated to various guilds, which assumed responsibility for casting, funding, and rehearsing.
    b. individual playlets were allocated to prominent families in York so that playwrighting and production stayed within a family tradition.
    c. all forty-eight were under the jurisdiction of a single appointed town official called the Master of Revels.
    d. all plays were subject to censorship by Church officials, who frequently expurgated humorous scenes.
    106

18. Which of the following is NOT true of the numerological features of the York Corpus Christi plays?
    a. The number of plays is twice the hours in the day.
    b. The annunciation of Christ's coming occurs one-quarter of the way through the overall drama.
    c. The Crucifixion-Resurrection occurs three-quarters of the way through the sequence.
  * d. The number "48" reflects the number of wounds on Christ's back.
    107

19. How much time did one complete production of the Corpus Christi plays last?
    a. The entire production, which took place in the afternoon light, lasted throughout all of Holy Week.
    b. Because the cycle was never performed in its entirety in one sitting, a complete production required one full liturgical year.
  * c. The production took almost an entire day, beginning at four-thirty in the morning and lasting until late in the evening.
    d. The entire production was conducted to last three days, with sixteen playlets performed each day beginning at 8 A.M.
    107

20. A four- or six-wheeled cart with a curtained dressing room below and an acting space above with at least two vertical levels for acting was called
    a. the guild hall float.
    b. an *arrière de corps.*
  * c. a pageant wagon.
    d. the dramatic cart.
    107

21. Although the secular theater died with the fall of Rome, which aspects of this tradition persisted during the Dark Ages?
  * a. minstreling, juggling, and "mumming"
    b. joke-telling and puppetry
    c. dancing, choral odes, and group recitations
    d. bawdy gestures, non-speaking actors, and the use of pig-bladders to carry artificial blood, used especially during the Crucifixion
    110

22. How many playlets comprise the York cycle?
    a. 24
    b. 33
    c. 60
  * d. 48
    112

23. What characterized the verse form of the York cycle?
    a. It was written in unrhymed iambic pentameter.
    b. It follows purely natural speech rhythms.
  * c. It is written with an irregular meter but an extraordinary amount of alliteration.
    d. It was written as a sonnet sequence.
    112

24. The verse of the medieval theatre
* a. was created for purpose of religious instruction.
  b. was created to add a musical aspect to everyday language.
  c. was created to enhance the memorization of lines.
  d. was created in the interests of showing likeness to everyday language.
  113

25. "Hellmouth" was
  a. drawn on the wall of the pageant wagon to represent the entrance to hell.
* b. a stage piece designed to "swallow" sinners into the low staging area.
  c. the central theme of the playlet of The Fall.
  d. a liturgical trope, like *Quem Queritas,* which was performed the first day of Lent.
  116

26. Which of the following is NOT true of the relationship between *Prometheus Bound* and the York cycle play?
  a. Both cultures feature this drama at an outdoor springtime festival associated with religious worship and celebration.
  b. Both dramas imply an awareness of man's potential to obey the laws laid down by religious revelation.
  c. Both dramas deal with the struggle of one character to break free from the restraints imposed by a higher authority.
* d. Both plays show God as rational and logical force for order.
  118

27. *Hubris* means
  a. submission brought on by succumbing to authority.
* b. wanton arrogance.
  c. the nobility of tragic suffering.
  d. adventuresome recklessness.
  118

28. How did medieval drama represent man's quest for individual knowledge?
* a. as a threat to religious and revealed truth
  b. as the only antidote to a long history of religious warfare
  c. as part of God's plan for human beings to take dominion over nature in the same way that Adam was given stewardship of the Garden
  d. as a form of striving that was ultimately irrelevant in the ordered cosmos described by the Great Chain of Being
  119

29. "Iconographic" means
  a. warlike.
  b. ironic.
* c. highly symbolic.
  d. humorous.
  120

30. Which aspect of the drama was most important to medieval performers?
    a. realism and historical accuracy
    b. beautiful language and poetry
    c. the artistry of the physical stage
    * d. the message of the play
    121

31. The playlet of the Crucifixion is central to the York cycle because
    a. numerically it occurs in the middle of the sequence and therefore carries metaphysical associations.
    * b. it stands at the center of a tonal shift in the playlets, mediating the despair of the previous plays with the hopefulness of the subsequent plays.
    c. it offers the principal actor, who played God, an opportunity to take a break before continuing in a more highly energized role.
    d. it was placed at a climax in the day, allowing the audience to go home and rest before the next playlet in the series appeared.
    122–123

32. The overall theme of the cycle plays was
    * a. the promise of man's salvation through God's intervention.
    b. the lesson that the biblical God was a powerful and strong one and best addressed from the standpoint of fear and dread.
    c. that the Christian God was ultimately very similar to the Greek gods; thus all cultures should be understood in the context of their universal values.
    d. that the quest of individual humanity to find value in the world was one that could be conducted only without the direct intervention of God.
    123

33. The central difference between Prometheus and Christ is that Prometheus suffers from principle but Christ suffers from
    a. nobility.
    * b. love.
    c. obedience to his father.
    d. guilt.
    123

34. Other medieval plays that are usually held up as excellent examples of medieval drama are
    a. *Ralph Roister Doister* and *The Slough of Despond.*
    b. *Pilgrim's Progress, Pilgrim's Decline,* and *Pilgrim's Salvation.*
    c. *The Scarlet Wound* and *Miserare Mei, Deus.*
    * d. *The Second Shepherd's Play* and *Everyman.*
    126

35. The difference between a trope and a drama relies upon the use of
    * a. impersonation in the drama.
    b. the church setting for tropes.
    c. the use of props in drama.
    d. the use of music and singing in liturgical tropes.
    102

36. "Trope" comes from the Latin word *tropus,* meaning
    a. metaphor.
    b. miracle.
  * c. added melody.
    d. holy song.
    102

37. The cycle plays were extraordinary not only because they were literary works written in the English language but also because their staging was unique in that it employed
    a. the platform stage.
    b. the proscenium arch.
  * c. the rolling procession.
    d. the traveling mime.
    106

38. In which Shakespearean play are the conventions and verse forms of medieval drama satirized?
    a. *Hamlet*
  * b. *A Midsummer Night's Dream*
    c. *Macbeth*
    d. *Pericles*
    114

39. According to George H. Szanto, the Wakefield cycle reflects a Christianity that is
  * a. partisan conservative.
    b. liberal.
    c. egalitarian.
    d. elitist.
    126

40. The theatre of the Middle Ages was
    a. amateur.
  * b. professional in that it was created and supported by highly motivated professional artisans.
    c. professional in that all the actors were paid.
    d. amateur, although actors were reimbursed for the cost of costumes they made.
    106

41. The Corpus Christi plays began with
  * a. The Creation and the Fall of Lucifer.
    b. Adam and Eve.
    c. The Birth of Christ.
    d. The Resurrection of Christ.
    110

42. The contemporary analogy to the rolling procession of the cycle plays may be found in
    a.   the half-time show at football games.
*   b.   the Rose Bowl Parade.
    c.   the flea market or bazaar.
    d.   the rodeo.
    111

43. A form of language, used as an effective means of character portrayal in medieval drama, that allowed villainous characters to strut around and storm on the stage was
    a.   the soliloquy.
    b.   the aside.
*   c.   ranting.
    d.   singing.
    115

44. In the playlet The Fall of Man, taken from the York cycle, the serpent's temptation of Adam is represented as
*   a.   intellectual.
    b.   sensual.
    c.   economic.
    d.   spiritual.
    119

45. *Quem queritas* means:
    a.   Where are you going?
*   b.   Whom seek you?
    c.   Why do you exist?
    d.   Who made you?
    102

46. What costume did the characters in *Quem Queritas* wear?
    a.   They wore no costumes.
*   b.   The Marys wore copes and the angel an alb.
    c.   The Marys wore street clothes, but the angel had wings.
    d.   The angel wore street clothes, but the Marys wore blue cloaks.
    103

47. Dramatic material that was written into the official Catholic Church liturgy and was staged as part of regular church services during the medieval period between the tenth and twelfth centuries was known as
    a.   historiographical drama.
*   b.   liturgical drama.
    c.   conversion drama.
    d.   celebration drama.
    104

ESSAY QUESTIONS

48. Describe the contribution of the guilds to the development of medieval drama.

49. Compare and contrast the roles of God/gods in *Prometheus Unbound* and "The Creation."

50. Consider all forty-eight plays of the York cycle as a single play that tells the story of the fall and resurrection of humanity through Christ. Humanity, expressed as the common trait of Adam and Eve, Noah, etc., is the central protagonist of this drama. Would this play be a tragedy or a comedy? (Hint: Why does Dante call his epic poem *The Divine Comedy?*)

51. Analyze the characterization of human beings in any one of the cycle plays. To what extent are characters drawn as types or emblems of the human condition, and to what extent do we see representation of realistic human frailties and weaknesses?

52. Compare and contrast the ritual function of Greek drama with that of medieval drama.

53. How was the economic burden of play production handled in medieval drama?

54. How did the language of medieval plays contribute to the theme of the plays or to the intention that framed their performance?

Chapter 5

The Shakespearean Era

1. The Renaissance was characterized by which of the following?
*   a. a renewed interest in classical (Greek and Roman) civilization
    b. the vigorous revival of monastic scholasticism
    c. the repudiation of the discoveries of the New World
    d. a celebration of Oriental cultures, especially Indian
    127

2. Which of the following is NOT true of the Renaissance?
    a. The Renaissance first emerged in southern Europe during the 1400s.
    b. The Renaissance supplied the intellectual seed bed for humanism.
*   c. The Renaissance world view held that God, not man, was the measure of all things.
    d. The Renaissance was marked by great developments in art, conquest, social organization, and philosophy.
    128

3. Which playwright was NOT one of Shakespeare's contemporaries?
    a. Ben Jonson
    b. John Ford
    c. Christopher Marlowe
*   d. John Dryden
    128

4. "The Elizabethan Age" refers to
*   a. the reign of Elizabeth (1558–1603).
    b. the reign of Elizabeth and her father (1542–1603).
    c. an English law, passed in Elizabeth's lifetime, that held that it was illegal for a monarch to take the throne before the age of 25.
    d. the period of time ranging from the reign of Elizabeth I to the reign of Elizabeth II.
    129

5. "The Jacobean Era" refers to
    a. a mythological age often alluded to in medieval drama, as in *Camelot.*
    b. the historical period marked by the reign of Elizabeth and her son Jacob (1558–1642).
    c. a period of the literary revival of Old Testament themes.
*   d. the historical period marked by the reign of James I (1603–1625).
    129

6. The heyday of Shakespearean drama came to an end
    a. in 1616 with Shakespeare's death.
*   b. in 1642 with the Puritan revolution, which burned theatres to the ground.
    c. in 1650 with the most pernicious outbreak of the black death.
    d. in 1588 with the defeat of the Spanish Armada.
    129

7. Which of the following is true about London playhouses?
*   a. There were two kinds of theatres, public and private.
    b. London playhouses were all public theatres centered in the innyard.
    c. London playhouses were initially constructed to be public service buildings.
    d. All theatrical activity in London was routed to Stratford-upon-Avon.
    129

8. Which of the following is true of public theatres?
*   a. Public theatres were located outside the city limits.
    b. Public theatres originated in private homes inside the city limits.
    c. By law, public theatres could not be placed near any establishment employing animals in entertainment.
    d. By law, public theatres had to be within walking distance of pubs, cafes, or restaurants.
    129

9. What objections did the Puritans have to the theatres?
*   a. Moral objections: the Puritans objected to the lascivious plots within the drama and to the unsavory collection of wicked people attending the drama.
    b. Economic objections: the public theatres cost too much for the average Puritan to attend.
    c. Social objections: the theatrical season conflicted with the Puritan calendar of holidays and celebrations.
    d. Political objections: Puritans opposed the monarch's tendency to grant privilege to dramatists rather than to clerics.
    130

10. The tiring house was
*   a. a dressing room.
     b. a storage place beneath the stage.
     c. the seating area for merchants.
     d. the lounge for nobles.
     130

11. The cellarage
     a. was a room that contained the machines, like pulleys and cranes, used to change scenes.
*   b. was the space below the stage.
     c. was a projected semicanopy over the stage.
     d. was a strongbox used to safeguard all important theatrical documents, like manuscripts and deeds.
     130

12. Our knowledge of the architecture of The Globe theatre comes from all of the following EXCEPT
     a. postage stamp–sized engravings of The Rose, The Globe, and The Hope theatres on illustrated London maps.
*   b. an actor's description of The Fortune.
     c. building contracts for The Fortune and The Hope.
     d. a drawing by a foreign visitor.
     130

13. Excavations of The Rose theatre, discovered in 1989, reveal which of the following?
    * a. The Rose was shaped as a polygon with a perimeter about 74 feet in diameter.
    b. The stage was circular and had a circumference of 310 feet.
    c. The roof was placed on posts buried twelve feet into the ground.
    d. The Rose had four doors for entry and exit of groundlings.
    130–131

14. Which of the following is true of The Globe?
    a. The foundation of The Globe describes a perfect circle.
    * b. The shape of The Globe was rectangular or polygonal.
    c. No traces of The Globe have ever been found.
    d. The tiring house of The Globe is intact, preserved by the library that was built over it.
    130

15. "The boards" refers to
    * a. boards mounted on sawhorses used to make the stage.
    b. boards supporting the stage door.
    c. the wooden stairway from the upper stories used by actors for spectacular entrances and exits.
    d. the structure connecting stage levels of different heights, usually used for fight scenes.
    131

16. How did the Elizabethan innyard contribute to the growth of drama?
    * a. The U shape of the inn, combined with its two- or three-story height, made a natural playing space.
    b. Innkeepers and their servants served as actors and actresses when their business was sporadic.
    c. The inns permitted traveling acting companies to rest their horses.
    d. The inns were the only establishment out of the Puritan jurisdiction.
    131

17. Which playhouse was NOT a London public theatre?
    a. The Globe
    b. The Curtain
    * c. The Dome
    d. The Hope
    129

18. The "groundlings" were
    * a. spectators who stood in the yard.
    b. the dressers who helped the actors ready themselves for scenes.
    c. the ticket takers who collected the price of admission.
    d. the grooms who remained outside the theatre taking care of horses and dogs.
    131

19. What three architectural elements comprised the Elizabethan playhouse?
    * a. the trestle stage, the pageant wagon, and the innyard
    b. the stage, the proscenium arch, and the balcony
    c. the courtyard, the pageant wagon, and the orchestra pit
    d. the elevated backstage, the dropping curtain, and the stage lights
    132

20. Which of the following is true of Shakespeare's playwrighting?
    a. Shakespeare wrote according to the rules of art formalized by Alexander Pope.
    b. Shakespeare composed his plays in accordance with Aristotelian principles of the unities.
  * c. Shakespeare was not governed by a formal aesthetic for writing.
    d. Shakespeare composed his plays in accordance with The Queen's Aesthetic Review.
    132

21. Shakespeare produced his plays
    a. at The Globe only.
    b. at The Globe, The Theatre, and The Curtain.
    c. at The Globe and in private theatres.
  * d. at The Globe, The Theatre, and The Curtain, at private playhouses, and at court.
    132

22. What office was performed by the Master of Revels?
  * a. The Master of Revels, the queen's officer, oversaw royal entertainments.
    b. The Master of Revels, a theatrical employee, organized the selection of plays for the public theatre's playing season.
    c. The Master of Revels, a government appointee, prepared all dramatic manuscripts for processing by the City Licensing Board.
    d. The Master of Revels, a church appointee, reviewed all plays in order to make recommendations to Puritan church officials.
    133

23. Shakespeare's acting company
    a. resided at The Globe theatre during the fall.
    b. disbanded at the end of each playing season.
  * c. was also a touring company.
    d. was housed at the queen's court all year.
    133

24. Who owned the plays?
    a. Each playwright owned his own play.
  * b. Troupes of actors owned their plays, as magicians own rabbits.
    c. Plays were equally owned by the star actor and the dramatist.
    d. Plays were owned by the reigning monarch, the leading actor, and the playwright.
    134

25. In Shakespeare's time, women's parts were played
  * a. by male actors.
    b. by female actors.
    c. by anyone below the age of 14.
    d. by either male or female actors, as long as they were professionally licensed.
    134

26. Which of the following is true of Shakespeare's relationship with the King's Men?
  * a. Shakespeare was part owner of the troupe itself and of its real estate holdings.
    b. The King's Men mutinied against Shakespeare because of disagreement over the resolution of *King Lear.*
    c. The King's Men dissolved in 1614 in the middle of a scandal involving Shakespeare's bribing of critics.
    d. Shakespeare left this company at the queen's request in order to form the Chamberlain's Men.
    135

27. Which of the following is NOT true of the composition of the Lord Admiral's Men?
    a. Philip Henslowe was the manager/producer.
    b. Edward Alleyn was its celebrated tragic actor.
    c. Christopher Marlowe was its playwright.
  * d. Will Kemp was its chief clown.
    135

28. Which of the following is NOT true of the Chamberlain's Men?
    a. The company was formed under the rule of Queen Elizabeth.
    b. The company came under the patronage of James I.
    c. The company changed its name to the King's Men.
  * d. The company was disbanded at Shakespeare's death.
    135

29. After The Globe was destroyed by fire in 1613,
    a. the theatrical company took up residence at The Theatre.
  * b. the theatrical company rebuilt The Globe.
    c. the theatrical company disbanded, and Shakespeare returned to Stratford.
    d. the theatrical company resided at James's court and were given full playing privileges in the palace.
    135

30. Which of the following is NOT true of the shift from medieval to Renaissance drama?
    a. Medieval rural settings were supplanted by vast geographic scenes.
    b. Morality plays were supplanted by tales of discovery, excitement, and awe.
    c. Regular rhyming was supplanted by natural language patterns.
  * d. Domestic themes dealing with the family were intensified.
    136

31. Before Shakespeare's rise to prominence as an English playwright, the English theatre scene was characterized by which of the following?
    a. There were no major English playwrights before Shakespeare.
    b. Only religious drama was permitted to be staged.
  * c. Contemporary playwrights wrote plays set in distant places for the public theatre.
    d. Playwrights wrote skits or masques for production in private homes.
    136

32. Which play has an entire scene written in French?
*   a. *Henry V*
     b. *Henry VIII*
     c. *Richard II*
     d. *Cambises*
     137

33. What pair of events marks the span of English Renaissance drama?
*   a. the first production of Preston's *Cambises* in 1561 to the onset of civil war in 1642
     b. the birth of Petrarch in the thirteenth century to the death of Shakespeare in 1616
     c. the printing of the first book in English in 1474 to the beheading of Charles II in 1649
     d. the production of the Corpus Christi plays in 1490 to the death of James I in 1625
     137

34. Which of the following is true of the status of printed plays in Shakespeare's time?
*   a. Original published versions of the plays bear little resemblance to the annotated versions commonly seen today.
     b. Original published versions of the plays are nearly identical to the versions commonly seen today.
     c. Original published versions of the plays were entirely handwritten.
     d. No original published versions of the plays exist.
     137

35. In Shakespeare's time, copyright law
     a. was strictly formulated and consistently enforced.
*   b. was nonexistent.
     c. was strictly defined but enforced only when challenged by writers.
     d. was ill defined but rigorously enforced when brought to trial.
     137

36. The first writer to supervise the publication of his own writing was
*   a. Ben Jonson.
     b. Christopher Marlowe.
     c. George Peele.
     d. Philip Henslowe.
     139

37. The Folio edition of Shakespeare's plays was edited by
*   a. two shareholders and actors in his company.
     b. Shakespeare's wife, Ann Hathaway.
     c. Shakespeare's son, Hamnet.
     d. the Master of Revels.
     139

38. Which of the following were NOT a typical kind of English Renaissance drama?
     a. tragedies, comedies, tragicomedies
     b. chronicle histories
     c. court masques
*   d. operas
     139

39. Blank verse is
   * a. unrhymed iambic pentameter.
   b. natural speech flow.
   c. poetry in which the persona of the narrator is not disclosed.
   d. a device by which poets freely join words in order to reduce metrical stress.
   139

40. In Shakespeare's time, costuming
   a. strictly conformed to the time and theme of the play.
   b. was not considered a significant aspect of the drama.
   * c. while splendid, reflected no concern for historical realism.
   d. reflected the conventions of classical theatre.
   140

41. The soliloquy is
   * a. a speech addressed directly to the audience.
   b. a speech recited by an actor in disguise.
   c. a form of dialogue between the principal actor and his beloved.
   d. a speech that other characters can hear although the actor believes that he is alone.
   141

42. How many plays did Shakespeare write?
   a. none
   * b. 37
   c. 39
   d. 15 by himself and 19 in collaboration
   143

43. Which of the following is true of the plays attributed to Shakespeare?
   a. Only five plays exist in the poet's own hand.
   b. One-third of the plays are incomplete.
   c. The quartos written before 1599 were collaborative works.
   * d. The division of plays into genres was an editor's choice, not Shakespeare's.
   143

44. Which of the following is true about *Romeo and Juliet?*
   a. Shakespeare wrote the only version of this story.
   * b. Shakespeare took the story from an English translation of an Italian writer.
   c. Shakespeare heard this story from traveling poets who had arrived from Italy.
   d. The love story was derived from a Latin account about the founding of Rome.
   143–144

45. The "Chorus" in *Romeo and Juliet* is
   a. a group of people who speak as one.
   b. a crowd with no speaking parts.
   * c. a single actor uninvolved in the action.
   d. two male actors speaking in concert.
   144

46. Which of the following offers an example of dramatic irony?
  * a. Romeo says that Juliet looks as if she is alive and she is, in fact, alive.
    b. Mercutio's Queen Mab speech
    c. Friar Lawrence's epilogue
    d. Tybalt breaks up the party with his accusation against Romeo.
    159

47. Which of the following is NOT an instance of Renaissance drama?
    a. Shakespeare's theatre in England
    b. the Spanish public theatre under Lope de Vega
    c. Italian *comedia dell'arte*
  * d. the French neoclassical theatre built upon tennis courts
    161

48. Which of the following does NOT characterize the *commedia dell'arte?*
  * a. written scripts actors committed to memory
    b. performances built around a *scenario*
    c. stock characters and set physical business
    d. whimsical masks and costumes
    161

49. Which of the following is NOT found among the stock characters of the *commedia dell'arte?*
    a. the young lovers, innamorato and innamorata
    b. the braggart soldier, Capitano
    c. the pompous academician, Dottore
  * d. the suffering mother, Mater Dolorosa
    161

50. Stock bits of clownish action in the *commedia dell'arte* were called
  * a. *lazzi.*
    b. *intermezzo.*
    c. *palazzo.*
    d. *aria.*
    162

51. The influence of the *commedia dell'arte* may be seen in which of the following?
    a. the pageant wagon of medieval miracle plays
  * b. the Punch and Judy of English puppet theatre
    c. the contemporary use of the soliloquy
    d. the recognition scene in German romantic drama
    162

ESSAY QUESTIONS

52. Briefly describe the transition from medieval to Renaissance staging.

53. (More advanced version of the same) Briefly describe the transition from medieval to Renaissance staging. Choose a scene from *Romeo and Juliet* that is not treated in this text (or choose a scene from another Shakespearean play), and explain, in the context of your previous description, how medieval and Renaissance staging accommodate this scene.

54. In *Romeo and Juliet,* Shakespeare presents us with scenes of great festivity and ceremony, which he balances with more quiet scenes using soliloquies, monologues, or dialogues. The orchestration of scenes is one way that the playwright balances the tension and rhythm of the drama.

    Pick three scenes from a different play (or three scenes from *Romeo and Juliet* that are not discussed in this chapter), and discuss the shifts in tempo, not only in staging but in language.

55. When Romeo and Juliet meet, their lines take the form of a sonnet. In dramatic terms, this poetic meeting creates the effect of a spotlight on the characters. What would the other characters be doing onstage? Explain three different ways you could stage the scene of Romeo and Juliet's meeting in order to accommodate the "stop" in time that the sonnet creates.

56. Define and explicate the function of dramatic irony in *Romeo and Juliet.*

57. Discuss the influence of the Church in Renaissance theatre history.

58. How did economic and political forces shape the growth and development of the Elizabethan playhouse?

Chapter 6

Kabuki—and the Theatre of Asia

1. Which of the following is true of theatre in Asia?
   a. There was no theatre as such.
   * b. A diverse tradition existed in Asian theatre.
   c. Asian theatre imitated and reshaped Western forms.
   d. Western theatre took its plots from an Asian tradition that preceded it by three thousand years.
   164

2. The most comprehensive and detailed theatrical treatise of the ancient world is
   * a. the Sanskrit *Natya Sutra,* or Doctrine of Dramatic Art (begun in the second century A.D.).
   b. *Kalidasa Kundalini,* the Zen of drama (written in Indonesia in 11 B.C.).
   c. *Tan Tien,* the handbook of the Peking Opera (transmitted orally for hundreds of years but written down by Portuguese priests in the twelfth century A.D.).
   d. the *Kabuki Nehru,* written for directors and actors in Japan in 2000 B.C.
   164

3. Which of the following is NOT true of Asiatic theatre?
   a. Asian theatre is never just "spoken"; it is danced, chanted, mimed, and very often sung.
   b. Asian theatre is more visual and sensual than literary or intellectual.
   c. Most Asians would consider the act of reading a play—separate from seeing it in performance—an odd pastime.
   * d. Asian plots are built on escalating incidents, stunning reversals, crescendoing climaxes, and elaborate plot closures.
   164

4. What do the *khon* mask theatre of Thailand, the *wayang wong* dance drama of Java, and the *kamyonguk* mask-dance of Korea have in common?
   a. They have all been the basis for Western forms of *cinéma vérité.*
   * b. They are still presented as part of agricultural rituals throughout the Asian countryside.
   c. They all use women as the main character in a conflict about patriarchal authority.
   d. These forms were devised as part of a festivity surrounding human sacrifice.
   165

5. Virtually all Kabuki actors in modern Japan can trace their familial and professional lineage
   a. to their actor-mothers and actor-grandmothers.
   b. through the bestowed favor of an emperor-king who granted them semidivine status in the sixteenth century.
   c. through a spiritual community based on the teachings of the Tao, which maintained that righteous acting brought one closer to enlightenment than righteous living.
   * d. to their actor-fathers and actor-grandfathers.
   166

6. Which of the following is true about the origin of Kabuki, one of the great historical theatre forms? Kabuki

* a. was created in Shakespeare's time and reached something of a zenith during Japan's shogun-dominated Edo period (1616–1853).
   b. grew out of the common mythology of Thespis, originally a Greek figure whose archetype found form in India, Indonesia, China, and Japan.
   c. was a relatively new art form whose roots correspond with the advent of Europeans in Japan.
   d. was originally an Indonesian art form that was carried via China through two hundred years of warfare between China and Japan.

166

7. Kabuki flowered during a period

* a. when Japan was completely isolated from all foreign influence, and thus it functions as an autonomous art form.
   b. when European influence began to touch Asia, and thus it reveals the happy blend of European tradition with Asian elements.
   c. before Greek civilization had come to exist, when the dominant culture of the world was divided among diverse European tribes and Huns.
   d. at the same time a related form flourished in China and southeast Asia.

166

8. The word *kabuki*

* a. derives from *kabuku,* meaning "tilting" or "askew," and refers to a style of behavior that might today be called "hip" or "punk."
   b. derives from *kabu,* meaning "intoxicated," and refers to the drugs used by men and women during the performance to achieve a state of enlightened consciousness.
   c. derives from the word *kab kab,* an onomatopoetic word reflecting the sound of wooden sandals on a stage, an allusion to the origin of the kabuki in the eleventh-century vogue of extreme footwear.
   d. means "fan" and refers to the central prop in Kabuki theatre, used by men and women alike as a vehicle to express a range of emotions and passions.

166

9. In its early forms, Kabuki was

   a. an elegiac, choral production performed by elderly men and women to celebrate the cultural history of the clan or tribe.
   b. a stylized court entertainment permitted only by upper-class nobles, none of whom could be foreigners, during designated times of the sacred calendar.
* c. more an erotic dance and fashion show than a drama, featuring an all-woman cast in short musical skits in which women played both male and female parts.
   d. a series of skits that grew up among the shopkeepers and nomads in the spring when the two groups met to exchange news and the fruits of harvest or pillage.

166

10. Kabuki was invented by
    a. a warlord to celebrate his wedding in 1240.
 * b. a Kyoto shrine maiden, Izumo Okuni, around 1600.
    c. an itinerant soldier and his troupe from India.
    d. the gods, as a form sacred to them, through which their wrath could be appeased.
    166

11. By the end of the seventeenth century, Kabuki
    a. had declined and was not played at all until the twentieth century.
    b. had been supplanted entirely by the puppet theatre.
    c. remained alive in the provinces as a marginal type of theatre.
 * d. had become a full-fledged dramatic medium with multi-act plays, magnificent costumes, scenery, and star performers.
    166

12. The new etymology for *kabuki,* reformulated by the end of the seventeenth century, was
 * a. *ka* (song) *bu* (dance) and *ki* (skill).
    b. *kabu* (fan) *ki* (dance).
    c. *kabukiyano* (I celebrate).
    d. *ka* (ghost) *buki* (procession).
    166

13. Which of the following is true about the status of the Kabuki playscript?
    a. Most Kabuki plays have a single author from a select family of authors who have handed down the tradition of writing for twenty generations.
 * b. Most Kabuki plays have multiple authors, some of them anonymous, and almost all the working scripts incorporate improvisations and alterations that actors have interpolated over the years.
    c. Most Kabuki plays have a single author who acquires performance experience through a system of open submissions and competitions.
    d. Most Kabuki plays are co-authored by two to six members of different guilds who collaborate to produce a piece that accurately represents all the castes of persons in the drama.
    167

14. Which of the following is not a type of Kabuki drama?
    a. history plays (*jidaimono,* or period things)
    b. domestic plays (*sewamono,* or "trouble things")
    c. dance-dramas (*shosagoto*)
 * d. woman's woes plays (*onnagata dono,* or "mother's tears")
    167–168

15. What was the first Nō drama adapted for Kabuki?
    a. *Kagami Jishi,* "the Lion Dance," in the nineteenth century
 * b. *Kanjincho,* by Ichikawa Danjuro VII in 1840
    c. *Misumi,* by Takae Susumu in 1929
    d. *Shogun,* by James Michener in 1985
    169

16. Which of the following is NOT a Kabuki theatre paired with its home city?
    a. Kabuki-za in Tokyo
    b. Shinkabuki-za in Osaka
    c. Minami-za in Kyoto
  * d. Fundoshi-za in Tokyo
    169

17. Which of the following is NOT true of Kabuki history plays?
    a. They dramatize in spectacular fashion major political events of the remote past drawn from different dynasties.
    b. The historical distance is little more than a protective cover for playwrights and actors who were in fact reflecting—under the guise of an apparently historical depiction—upon various controversial issues of nobles and political officials of their own time.
  * c. Based on their clear meaning, history plays were devised as a teaching tool to transmit culture to generations of schoolchildren.
    d. History plays are spectacular.
    168

18. Kabuki's greatest playwright was
    a. Izumon Okuni.
  * b. Chikamatsu Monzaemon.
    c. Shogun Taipei.
    d. Chatto matto Kudasai.
    169

19. Which of the following is NOT true about the relationships between Japanese society and the Kabuki drama?
    a. By 1629, the Kabuki had become so entwined with prostitution that the Japanese government outlawed women from the stage.
    b. Because many domestic Kabuki dramas end in suicide, or double suicide, the government attempted to ban such plays as they led to real suicides in consequence.
    c. Because catamites (attractive boy prostitutes) were hired to perform Kabuki, the Japanese government, by 1652, outlawed boy actors, requiring adult male performers to shave their forelocks to demonstrate an elderly (and non-erotic) appearance.
  * d. Because many Kabuki plays were highly charged political satires, the government initiated a series of highly restrictive censorship laws, a few of which remain in effect today.
    166, 169

20. What is true about the performance schedule of Kabuki?
  * a. In previous centuries, Kabuki was an all-day affair that started at dawn, with the audience shuttling back and forth between tea houses and the stage house until the play's end late in the day.
    b. In previous centuries, Kabuki plays began at dusk and continued late into the evening, where the shadows thrown by the paper lanterns had an important role in representing character and audience, and the long playing time necessitated the audience's carrying snacks with them to last through the night.

c. In previous centuries, Kabuki was played on a makeshift stage in an open-air theatre; performances, from noon to dusk, were carried over for a week.

d. In previous centuries, Kabuki was performed on the steps of temples as a prelude to the worship or meditation activities that followed.

170

21. Which of the following is NOT true of the Kabuki-za stage?

    a. The auditorium is large (the Kabuki-za seats 2,600) and for the most part Western-styled, with seating in theatre chair rows that fill the main hall and the two balconies.

    b. The vast stage holds a proscenium 9 feet wide (twice the width of a standard Broadway stage) and an acting area 30 feet deep.

    c. The stage is abutted at stage right by a perpendicular runway, the *hanamichi* ("flower way"), which extends back through the audience.

*   d. Props and scenery, usually made of rice-paper, light wood, and screen paintings, are stored folded up in special compartments beneath the audience's seats.

170–171

22. The *shichi-san* (seven-three) is

*   a. a point seven-tenths of the distance toward the stage, which becomes a "hot spot" on the *hanamichi* for major speeches and tableaux.

    b. a dramaturgical convention that divides the performance into ten parts, with the climax occurring after the seventh and the denouement in the following three parts.

    c. a series of privileged seating, whereby the elite audience descended from the seven original shogunates and three gods may kneel on tatami mats, watch the performance, and drink tea.

    d. the conventional name given to the prologue at the opening of the play.

171

23. The Kabuki curtain (*hikimaku*), a famous symbol of Kabuki art, is

*   a. a lightweight cloth, comprised of alternating black, green, and rust-colored vertical stripes, that has been used since the seventeenth century, and that billows out in the breeze.

    b. a heavyweight fabric like carpet suspended on two bamboo rods that roll up and down through the use of a lever.

    c. a thematic design drawn on paper or canvas that represents in tableaux the major theme or characters of the play.

    d. a heavy carpet hung on strong metal poles with the ensign or device of the theatrical company woven in the center.

171

24. Kabuki scenery provides

*   a. a highly aesthetic and symbolic support of the play's narrative; it does not attempt to create realistic stage illusion.

    b. a realistic setting to support the creation of a whole play world.

    c. a blank slate, through a stripped set backed by bare screens, against which the events of the play "draw" the world view.

    d. a highly ornate set, decorated with gifts from public benefactors.

172

25. The first theatre to make use of revolving stages (1758), stage elevators (1727), and rolling stage wagons was
    a. Nō drama.
 * b. Kabuki drama.
    c. *shingeki.*
    d. Bunraku.
    172

26. Kabuki costumes are
 * a. based on the history of the period described, and for domestic plays, they are nominally realistic versions of appropriate period wear.
    b. handed down from generation to generation and used to represent stylized or typical characters.
    c. garments actually owned by the actors.
    d. donated by guilds with the guild name embroidered on them, much like modern-day baseball league uniforms.
    175

27. The name given to the raised music room with a slatted front wall at the far right of the procenium, behind which the orchestra plays, is
    a. *samisen.*
    b. *obi.*
    c. *ki.*
 * d. *geza.*
    172

28. Which of the following is NOT the surname of a Kabuki family?
    a. Nakamura
    b. Onoe
    c. Bando
 * d. Mishima
    172

29. *Iemoto* refers to
 * a. a rigid system ensuring the orderly succession of a family's actors, with fathers passing on their roles to sons, such that an acting student not from one of the families could no more become an actor than an emperor.
    b. the name of the cry given by the protagonist at the climax of the play.
    c. the white socks worn with *zoris* by Kabuki actors.
    d. the social privilege of boxed seats accorded to aristocrats and wealthy donors.
    172, 174

30. What is the name given to the female ideal type characterized by pinched-back shoulders held at a deferential tilt; a gait with knees bent and held together, toe pointing inward; a high-pitched, sweetly demure voice; and an extravagantly styled, geisha-like appearance, with chalk-white make-up, red lips, and eye liner?
     a. *aragato*
   * b. *onnagata*
     c. *wagoto*
     d. *kumadori*
     174–175

31. Of two principal male parts, which one is characterized by an outlandish exaggeration of the samurai—an outrageous caricature of machismo comprising a thunderous, deep voice; a high-stepping, arms-flailing deportment; an enormous costume with billowing sleeves, elevator clogs, and two long swords; and war-paint make-up?
   * a. *aragato*
     b. *onnagata*
     c. *wagoto*
     d. *kumadori*
     175

32. Kabuki actors must train
   * a. for much of their lives, working from small parts to larger ones, inheriting major roles in their forties, developing a "kabuki face" by their fifties.
     b. for ten years in colleges and graduate schools, starting with *koken* roles, then specializing in male or female types.
     c. by observing reality carefully under the tutelage of a spiritual instructor and by a habit of meditation, in groups or alone.
     d. in their twenties by taking declamation and dance classes, moving on to literature and philosophy classes in their thirties.
     176

33. Which male part, more realistic in speech than the "wild man" type, associated with the court city of Kyoto, wears whitened make-up, moves with refined delicacy and grace, and can be romantic but more often is effeminate and petulant?
     a. *aragato*
     b. *onnagata*
   * c. *wagoto*
     d. *kumadori*
     175

34. Which of the following is NOT true of the *koken?*
     a. They are dressed and veiled wholly in black and scurry onstage to help the actor through a costume change.
     b. They may hand the actor his props or straighten the actor's wig or costume after a dance.
     c. They are apprentices or understudies for the actors they serve.
   * d. They are actors in the play who take on a purely symbolic role.
     176

35. The *mie,* a sudden, grotesquely contorted freeze, ordinarily in an *aragato* character and requiring the actor to cross his eyes, turn his head sharply forward with the chin tucked in, and point a big toe skyward, expresses
* a. the emotional climax of a scene.
  b. foreshadowing of the death of the primary character.
  c. the actor's homage to the audience and the playwright.
  d. an undercutting humor directed at the other events or characters in the play.
  176

36. The actor's *yago* is
* a. the traditional name the actor adds to his legal name, representing the town and shop his family may have (or may not have) owned for several generations.
  b. the name given to the actor's wigs and make-up case and accessory box.
  c. the name given to the samurai's war-paint.
  d. the name given to the puppet-master's personal collection of puppets.
  178–179

37. Fight scenes, or *tachimawari,* are group *kata*
  a. played by trained gymnasts who specialize in this kind of acting early in their apprenticeships.
* b. stylized to a point where there is no contact between actors or weapons, so that when mortally wounded, the actor tumbles into a somersault and runs offstage.
  c. rendered realistically by regular cast members.
  d. requiring the onstage action to halt and the *koken* to intervene, assuming the part of a lead Kabuki actor, while the remaining actors begin a stylized dance.
  176

38. The *kakegoe* is the name given to
  a. the clappers that sound to announce the beginning of a performance.
  b. a special clapper, handled by a formally garbed musician, to accompany the victory *mie.*
* c. specific vocal encouragement given to favored actors by their fans to indicate approval.
  d. a cry of disapproval, like the Bronx cheer or jeer, the equivalent to shouting out "Ham."
  178

39. Which of the following is NOT a contemporary innovation in the Kabuki theatre?
  a. The theatre building is Westernized, with lobbies, proscenium arches, modern theatre seating, air conditioning, box offices, and public address systems.
  b. Kabuki lighting is Westernized except that the audience area remains fully lit during the performance.
  c. Contemporary music may be employed in some performances, like that of the New Kabuki.
* d. The curtain is formed of red heavyweight drapes, drawn aside and held in place with a braided gold rope.
  179

40. The Nō and Kyōgen are collectively called
    a. *samisen*
    b. *onnagata*
  * c. Nōgaku
    d. Bunraku
    180

41. Which of the following is true of the relationship between Nō and Kyōgen drama?
    a. Kyōgen is more revered and cerebral; Nō offers the comic relief.
    b. Kyōgen refers to the danced versions of Nō themes.
  * c. Nō is more revered and cerebral; Kyōgen is the comic relief.
    d. Kyōgen is mystical; Nō is realistic.
    180

42. A highly ceremonial musical and dance drama that is mysterious, tragic, and usually supernatural, of which 240 texts are produced today written by members of a single family about five hundred years ago, designed to be sung rather than spoken, characterizes which type of theatre?
    a. Kyōgen
    b. Kabuki
  * c. Nō
    d. Bunraku
    180–181

43. All Nō plays center on the *shite,*
  * a. a single character representing gods, ghost, woman, animal, or warren, played in a mask, who is prompted, or challenged, by a secondary character.
    b. the chorus.
    c. the interrogating character, played without a mask, who raises questions about the nature of the universe.
    d. a warrior figure, male or female, who embodies philosophical or religious virtue in a fight against the forces of evil.
    181–182

44. The *waki* is
    a. the name given to the samurai warrior in Kabuki.
  * b. a Nō character, always a living male human (usually a minister, commoner, or priest), played without a mask.
    c. the figure of the fool or trickster in Bunraku drama.
    d. a stylized female type, the suppliant woman, in Kabuki drama.
    181–182

45. Nō drama may be characterized by
   * a. a medieval, elliptical, or obscure language; a small cast; static and solemn action; and a glacial pace.
   b. lively conflict between characters, an action plot, and colloquial language.
   c. frequent ritualized songs, accompanied by a small, four-instrument orchestra, and free-form dance that is often improvised.
   d. a curt question-answer format, like a courtroom drama, in which topical issues are debated and in which members of the audience are invited to reply and at the end write down their "verdict" on the issue represented.
   182

46. Originally derived from medieval story-telling, puppet shows, and lute strumming, the Japanese puppet theatre is known as a
   a. Kyōgen.
   b. Nō.
   c. Bushmari.
   * d. Bunraku.
   167

47. *Kumadori* is the name given to
   a. the puppets in the Bunraku theatre.
   b. the assumed, falsetto voice of female characters in Kabuki.
   c. the victory *mie* given by the male lead in Kabuki.
   * d. the red, purple, and black facial war-paint worn by samurai types in Kabuki.
   175

48. The three-stringed, banjo-like instrument, plucked by an ivory plectum, that accompanies Kabuki performances is called a
   a. sitar.
   b. lute.
   c. *geza.*
   * d. *samisen.*
   172

49. If you attended a performance in which the only scenery was a single, gnarled pine, you would immediately understand that you were attending which kind of performance?
   a. Kabuki
   b. Bunraku
   c. Kyōgen
   * d. Nō
   181

50. If you attended a performance in which a series of painted, forward-rolling cylinders, used to depict the ocean with wavy black, blue, white, and gray lines, flowed between two houses of warring families to depict their estrangement, you would know you were attending which kind of performance?

 *   a.   Kabuki
     b.   Bunraku
     c.   Kyōgen
     d.   Nō
172

ESSAY QUESTIONS

51. Briefly characterize the Bunraku, Kabuki, and Nō dramas in terms of the stage design and how design supports or accompanies the performance.

52. Take a scene from a well-known Western play like *Macbeth,* and explain how it might be staged for a Kabuki-influenced performance. Make sure you account for character types, costumes, the nature of the language, possible places for the intervention of *koken,* and the staging of fight or romantic scenes. (For example, how might the *koken* be made an integral part in staging a scene from *Macbeth?*)

53. What is the significance of *kata* both in Japanese social life and in the theatre?

54. What is the role of the *koken* in Kabuki?

55. Characterize the different character types in Kabuki drama.

56. Provide a brief reprise of the history of Kabuki drama, and then, either by using other chapters from this book or by researching theatre history in the library, describe the state of theatre at parallel historical moments in Europe.

Chapter 7
The Royal Theatre

1. The period following the Renaissance, characterized by consolidation and refinement of creative energy and the imposition of rational sensibility and order, was called
   a. Baroque.
   b. the Restoration.
   c. Puritan rule.
 * d. the Enlightenment.
   183

2. The Enlightenment engendered all of the following EXCEPT
   a. the physical laws of Isaac Newton.
   b. the political and social analysis of Baron de Montesquieu.
   c. the rationalist philosophies of René Descartes, Immanuel Kant, and David Hume.
 * d. the architecture of Sir Christopher Wren.
   183

3. Which adjective, derived from the name of a god, originally referred to passionate revelry and uninhibited pleasure seeking and later came to be associated with the religious, omni-sensual or rhapsodic release of energy?
 * a. Dionysian
   b. Apollonian
   c. Mercurial
   d. Jovian
   184

4. Which adjective, derived from the name of a god, describes that which is beautiful, wise, and serene and later came to be associated with the imposition of order and form?
   a. Dionysian
 * b. Apollonian
   c. Mercurial
   d. Jovian
   184

5. Which court did NOT make important contributions to late-seventeenth-century drama?
   a. the Spanish court and hunting lodge of Philip IV
 * b. the court of Napoleon I and his consort, Desirée
   c. the English court of Charles II
   d. the English court of Charles I
   185

6. Molière once said, "The great test of your plays is . . ."
   a. "the money your plays bring in."
   b. "the number of women who cry at the end."
   c. "the kindness you persuade in others."
 * d. "the judgment of the Court."
   185

7. Who made up the French, English, and Spanish courts?
* a. a landed nobility drawn into the social circle of the king, composed of a wealthy and urbane intelligentsia, members of the emerging professional class of civil servants and lawyers, and a few members of the emerging bourgeoisie
   b. primarily members of the newly rich and powerful bourgeoisie in addition to a few successful writers, munitions makers, and the second-generation aristocracy
   c. a diverse group containing old nobility, newly monied merchants, and travelers and traders from other European and Oriental locations
   d. the king's family and retainers in addition to special merchants with royal contracts and occasionally a scholar or artist from abroad
   185–186

8. "Neoclassicism" describes
   a. a revival of Greek *kothurnoi.*
* b. the accepted dramaturgy of the Royal era.
   c. a style of theatre in which pillars supported the stage.
   d. a style of drama focusing on ideas rather than emotions.
   186

9. The critical foundation of neoclassical dramaturgy was
   a. the use of court costumes rather than costumes appropriate to the era.
   b. the extensive use of blood on the stage.
* c. the avoidance of stage violence and vigorous physical action.
   d. the use of vulgar speech particular to the streets.
   186

10. In the neoclassical era, Shakespeare was seen as
    a. a brilliant playwright for all ages.
*   b. somewhat primitive.
    c. the epitome of all drama.
    d. a puppet of the queen and writer of ideological plays.
    186

11. The rules of playwrighting came from
    a. Pope's "Essay on Man."
    b. Coleridge's "Principles of Genial Criticism."
    c. Sidney's "Defense of Poesy."
*   d. Aristotle's "Poetics."
    186

12. Neoclassical dramaturgy treated all of the following EXCEPT
*   a. organizing the changing of characters.
    b. dividing a play into acts and scenes.
    c. applying the proper metrics to verse.
    d. structuring the plot.
    186

13. The neoclassical unities included
    a. unity of place.
    b. unity of time only.
    c. unity of time, place, and action.
 * d. unity of time, place, action, and tone.
    186

14. Which of the following was NOT a principle of neoclassical dramaturgy?
    a. No tragedy was to sustain comic relief.
 * b. Heroes had to die onstage.
    c. No comedy could sustain moments of pathos.
    d. A verse pattern could not be altered in the course of the play.
    186

15. What happened to playwrights who violated the unities?
    a. Their plays were prohibited from performance, and the playwrights incurred a financial
       fine if they attempted to stage the plays in private.
 * b. Many spent the bulk of their time defending themselves in print, and many finally gave up
       writing altogether.
    c. Plays that violated the unities did not pass the approval of the Monsieur de la Théâtre,
       the French equivalent to the Master of Revels, and could not be licensed or produced
       at all.
    d. Many spent their own fortunes on private performances in individual homes and sent special
       invitations to lords in the hopes of securing noble patrons.
    186

16. A *divertissement* is
    a. a form of advertising using pamphlets, handwritten notes, or invitations and individual
       word-of-mouth.
 * b. a frothy entertainment designed solely for the diversion of the court, to be enjoyed and
       then forgotten.
    c. a card game popular with gamblers, often practiced before the theatre entertainment began.
    d. a type of drink made from anisette, rose water, and cloves that was served before the
       performance.
    196

17. Molière's *The Bourgeois Gentleman*
    a. celebrates the rising middle class.
 * b. is a popular social satire combining romance, social commentary, and farcical hijinks.
    c. is a comedy famous in Europe for its sublime metrics, its lofty theme, and its elevated
       portrayal of human nature.
    d. is a social commentary that exposes the injustice done to women by the middle class.
    196

18. Which of the following is true of the history of *The Bourgeois Gentleman?*
    a. Molière wrote the play when he was severely impoverished; he paid a lord to advance it to the king; and while it was not popular with the king, it came to the attention of nobles who staged it anyway and produced the clothiers riots.
    * b. It was commissioned by Louis XIV for a 1670 premiere at the royal chateau at Chambord and afterward became a public hit.
    c. It was originally written on the occasion of the German king's marriage to a commoner; while the play was flawed in German, Molière's translation into his own French language revealed the intrinsic merit of the drama and became beloved by the archbishop of Chantilly.
    d. Molière wrote this play when his future wife, ten years his senior, heard of the death of her first husband during the Frankish Anglican wars. Wanting to cheer her up, he wrote the play, which was then circulated among family members.
    196

19. Built for Cardinal Richelieu, this theatre was a tennis court-sized structure, measuring 108 x 36 feet, and was equipped with a proscenium arch. The galleries were set up like *jeu de paume* and contained an amphitheatre arrangement of stone steps that rose in the parterre across the stage. It was Molière's public home for most of his career.
    a. the Paris Opera House
    b. the Hippodrome
    * c. the Palais Royale
    d. the Théâtre du Côte du Chat
    196

20. A *ferme* is
    * a. a painted wing used to represent a side wall or backdrop.
    b. a sconce around the proscenium frame.
    c. a shuttered backdrop.
    d. a curtain raised and lowered for performances.
    197

21. The frontispiece to an edition of *The Bourgeois Gentleman* gives us a sense of its staging. A cherub's severed arm mounted like a stag's head on the angle wings provides what information about the relationship between scenery and the script?
    a. Monsieur Jourdain is a heretic.
    b. Cardinal Richelieu has taken over the house.
    * c. Monsieur Jourdain lacks taste.
    d. Monsieur Jourdain was very contemporary in his household decor.
    197

22. Which of the following is the precursor of the musical comedy of contemporary times?
    a. the operetta
    b. the neoclassical verse sung at court
    * c. the *divertissement*
    d. the *chanson de molineaux*
    197

23. What did money signify in the world and thus in the drama of seventeenth-century Europe?
    a. It symbolized the emphasis on the artificial trappings of the world and thus, like wigs and elaborate dress, was used to show the foppery of nobles.
*   b. It highlighted the differences between feigned values and intrinsic ones, between hollow presumption and flattery and solid worth.
    c. It symbolized access to the ruling class.
    d. It was seen in terms of economic determinism; who you were depended upon the amount of money you possessed; thus it was tied to notions of existential identity.
    207

24. One metatheatrical device that occurs in *The Bourgeois Gentleman* is
    a. witty dialogue.
    b. movable stage furniture.
    c. painted scenery.
*   d. the play-within-the-play.
    208

25. The *Mamamouchi* ceremony in *The Bourgeois Gentleman* is
*   a. the ritual investiture of Monsieur Jourdain in the gown and turban of a Turkish prince.
    b. the ritual bath or baptism Monsieur Jourdain forces his daughter to undergo before she can be married.
    c. the ritual exchange of blood through gentlemen's cutting their thumbs to signify brotherhood as a prelude to becoming business partners.
    d. a Christian ceremony used to reaffirm faith against the influence of the Turkish prince.
    209

26. The purpose of the *Mamamouchi* ceremony in *The Bourgeois Gentleman* is to
    a. symbolize and celebrate the king's religious conversion.
*   b. enchant a court faddishly fascinated with the Orient.
    c. foreshadow a marriage at the close of the play.
    d. show the intrinsic moral weakness of Monsieur Jourdain when he schemes to take a mistress.
    210

27. Molière died in 1673, when he
    a. was beheaded by the king for his satire against royalty in *Tartuffe.*
    b. faded into oblivion and died from typhoid in the home of his upholsterer father.
*   c. had a convulsion while acting in his own play, *The Imaginary Invalid;* although he finished the performance, he died afterward.
    d. was thrown from a horse on his way to see a performance written by a rival playwright.
    210

28. "The Restoration" refers to
    a. the return of English lands to the landed gentry who had lost them during the reign of Cromwell.
*   b. the restoration of the English monarch after a period of revolution and Puritan domination.
    c. the restoration of English as the national language after a period of time during which Latin and French were seen as the universal languages of the day.
    d. the rebuilding of London after it had been burned to the ground in the great fire of 1665.
    211

29. During which period of time were dramatic performances banned and theatres burned to the ground?
 * a. from the Civil War in 1642 to the reign of Charles II in 1660
   b. during the Napoleonic Wars
   c. during the papacy of Clement VI
   d. during the American Revolution
   211

30. The first two theatres chartered by Charles II in England were
   a. built on the foundation and in the image of the Elizabethan playhouse.
   b. converted from buildings normally used for civil servants.
 * c. converted tennis courts.
   d. remodeled salons in the king's palace.
   211

31. The *jeu de paume* style refers to theatres that were
   a. polygonal with a thrust stage.
 * b. converted tennis courts.
   c. derived from the practice of playing in innyards that led to theatre-in-the-round.
   d. a return to the staging practices of medieval drama based on the parallelism between the stage and the front of the church.
   211

32. Which of the following was NOT an improvement made by the Restoration stage over the stage of the Royal theatre?
   a. The Restoration pit was raked to slope toward the stage and was lined with rows of backless benches.
 * b. Standing room in the pit became the latest fashion.
   c. The stage was raked, enhancing the perspective of flat wing and border scenery.
   d. A large apron was built to project into the audience.
   211, 213

33. The English Restoration drama audience was
   a. unlike the French, in that the audience was composed of middle-class people.
 * b. like the audience of the French Royal theatre, composed of a club of self-selecting luminaries.
   c. unlike the French audience, composed only of the king and nobles.
   d. like the French, more interested in political satire than in psychodrama.
   211

34. Who was the famous Italian stage designer who brought technologies to Paris in 1645, converting the Petit Bourbon and the Palais Royale to mechanically sophisticated theatres?
 * a. Giacomo Torelli
   b. Almos Pirandello
   c. Leonardo da Pisa
   d. Alfredo Lam
   209

35. How did Restoration acting troupes differ from Renaissance acting troupes?
* a. In the Restoration, women could act.
 b. Understudies became common during the Restoration.
 c. Restoration actors needed extensive musical training.
 d. Restoration troupes did not require that the age of the actor match the age of the character.
 213

36. Which of the following was NOT a typically Restoration genre?
 a. heroic and neoclassical tragedies
 b. tragicomedies
 c. comedies and musical entertainments
* d. musical comedy
 213

37. The great masterpiece of Restoration comedy is
 a. John Dryden's *All for Love.*
* b. William Congreve's *The Way of the World.*
 c. Aphra Behn's *The Rover.*
 d. John Milton's *L'Allegro.*
 214

38. Molière's patron, the Sun King, was
* a. Louis XIV.
 b. Louis XVI.
 c. Louis XV.
 d. Louis Roi.
 195

39. In *The Way of the World,* which character speaks the strongest appeal for female freedom in marriage?
 a. Mirabell
* b. Millamant
 c. Lady Wishfort
 d. Witwould
 216

40. In addition to her celebrity as a Restoration actress, Nell Gwynne was also known as
 a. a celebrated playwright.
 b. a wealthy woman who wisely invested her assets in foreign land ventures.
* c. the mistress of Charles II.
 d. a member of Parliament.
 213

41. A contemporary account of the Restoration theatre is available to us from
* a. the diaries of Samuel Pepys.
 b. Boswell's *Life of Johnson.*
 c. extant theatre reviews and gossip columns from London diaries.
 d. diaries of Russian aristocrats traveling in England.
 213

42. Which of the following is one of Molière's "machine plays"?
    a. *Tartuffe*
    b. *The Bourgeois Gentleman*
    c. *The Misanthrope*
  * d. *Amphitryon*
    209

43. During which period did dramatic criticism come into its own?
  * a. during the Restoration
    b. during the Renaissance
    c. at the beginning of the nineteenth century
    d. 1765
    187

44. Molière's dramaturgy shows the influence of which classical playwright?
  * a. Terence
    b. Plautus
    c. Sophocles
    d. Aeschylus
    195

45. *Jeu de paume* was
  * a. a game like handball that was eventually played with racquets.
    b. a horse race over a short distance.
    c. a ritual conducted before harvesting apples.
    d. a hand in poker.
    190

46. Killigrew's Theatre Royal in Drury Lane was designed by
    a. Peter Street.
    b. Samuel Johnson.
    c. Inigo Jones.
  * d. Christopher Wren.
    211

47. Who was the first Englishwoman to earn her living as a playwright?
    a. Good Queen Bess
    b. Lady Aurora Sidney
  * c. Aphra Behn
    d. Frances Wadsworth
    188

48. Congreve's play is considered a masterpiece for
  * a. its brilliant combination of perfectly honed dialogue with an incisive portrayal of the manners and values of the Restoration aristocracy.
    b. the most exotic combination of costume, dance, and music ever seen in an English comedy.
    c. its sustained and serious treatment of social problems.
    d. its incisive picture of the torment attending kingship in a world where the monarchy has been threatened from within and from without.
    214

ESSAY QUESTIONS

49. In *The Bourgeois Gentleman,* Molière uses the contrast between a character's self-importance and the importance that other people project on him. To what extent does money mediate the exchange? To what extent does Monsieur Jourdain function like a playwright in producing and performing the spectacle of himself? Is it more important, in this play world, to *appear* to be rich than actually to *be* rich?

50. Consider the relationships in *The Way of the World* and *The Bourgeois Gentleman.* Both of these worlds celebrate appearances in their thematic treatment of the play. Discuss the configuration of relationships in the two plays. How do the two plays relate to authority?

51. Analyze the marriage contract in *The Way of the World.* What does such an agreement imply about the status of women? Do women in Molière's plays have the same type of freedom as English women?

52. What is "the way of the world"? How do Millimant and Mirabell fit into it?

53. Using your knowledge both of Molière's life and his work, explain the importance of the court to his art.

54. Summarize the theatrical and political history that led to the adoption of the *jeu de paume* configuration of staging.

Chapter 8
The Modern Theatre: Realism

1. According to Freud, the human animal could be explained or understood in a person's direct response to the prompts of
    a. the id.
    b. the superego.
    * c. the Unconscious.
    d. the superego.
    221

2. According to Karl Marx, all human behavior has its origin in
    a. the struggle for survival, which leads to competition for food and sex.
    * b. economic greed, class struggle, and primal amorality.
    c. the conflicting drives of love and death, which create a conflict in the psyche.
    d. an awareness of a higher spiritual dimension beyond the pale of human experience.
    221

3. Realist theatre has its roots in
    a. the elaboration and refinement of neoclassical elements.
    b. nostalgia for Greek aesthetics.
    c. an ironic attitude applied to medieval theatre.
    * d. a revolt against the artifice of neoclassical form.
    223

4. Besides an aesthetic overhaul, the realist theatre carried another agenda:
    * a. rebellion against contrived manners contributed toward a theatre with a distinctly democratic, anti-Royalist air.
    b. the refinement of neoclassical aesthetics supported an elitist intellectual politics.
    c. the reinstatement of God/gods as fully empowered characters reasserted metaphysical significance to humanity's meaningless existence.
    d. scientific agendas were promulgated through the use of hi-tech stage machinery, special effects, and body doubles.
    223

5. The earliest phase of realism was called
    * a. naturalism.
    b. scientism.
    c. romanticism.
    d. mesmerism.
    223

6. What sensibility was embodied in romantic drama?
*   a. Romanticism attempted to re-activate passion, which, critics argued, had been dormant since Shakespeare.
    b. Reason and order prevailed at the expense of passion to make romantic theatre more restrained and more polished than its neoclassical antecedents.
    c. Reason and passion were both subsumed to the importance of the dream state.
    d. Moral education, rather than the animation of any human emotion, remained paramount.
    223

7. Which of the following is NOT a romantic work?
    a. Goethe's *Faust,* Part II
    b. Schiller's *The Robbers*
    c. Rostand's *Cyrano de Bergerac*
*   d. Lope de Vega's *El Cid*
    224

8. The free-form picaresque stories, exotic locales, grotesque heroics, and sprawling dramatic structure of romanticism gave rise to a theatre that survives today in the form of
    a. cinema.
*   b. grand opera.
    c. novels.
    d. intermezzi.
    224

9. What architectural contribution did the romantic period make to theatre?
    a. the universal adoption of the thrust stage
    b. the European adoption of the arena stage
*   c. in England and America, the universal adoption of the proscenium theatre
    d. the English and French adoption of theatre-in-the-round
    224

10. The primary goal of realism was
*   a. likeness to life.
    b. social commentary.
    c. social satire.
    d. the evocation of the dream state.
    224

11. Realism excluded all of the following EXCEPT
    a. prettified settings and contrived endings.
*   b. characters drawn true to life and subject to their individual social states.
    c. dramatic conventions and abstractions.
    d. stylized costumes and performances.
    224

12. One convention of the realist theatre was that dialogue
    a. stood for conversation.
    * b. was conversation.
    c. revealed philosophical truths.
    d. symbolized abstract ideals.
    224

13. Realism explored the social, political, and psychological aspects of human life through every aspect of stage production EXCEPT
    a. playwrighting: the genres were blended, climaxes were flattened, and certainties were derided.
    b. stage design: scenery depicted ordinary living environments that were as messy as their real-life counterparts.
    c. characterization: characters were drawn from everyday life.
    * d. plot: plot still retained its emphasis on dramatic action, especially the highly clarified decisions of state.
    226

14. Which of the following is NOT true of realist drama?
    a. Genres were blended.
    b. Scenery depicted ordinary living environments that were as messy as their real-life counterparts.
    * c. Dramatic characters emerged from high-class social strata: kings and princes.
    d. Doubts, muddles, and confusions became the principal actions of realistic plays.
    226

15. The new hero of realist drama was
    a. unquestioningly confident in his or her own might no matter how great the opposing forces.
    * b. perplexed and inarticulate in the face of myriad forces fighting for control of his or her soul.
    c. passionate and high-strung in his or her quest for idealist causes.
    d. intellectual, rational, and self-aware and always striving for the balance in decisions of geopolitical importance.
    226

16. Realism was
    a. only aesthetic.
    b. only social.
    * c. a political and aesthetic force.
    d. entertainment.
    226

17. Which of the following characterizes realist drama?
    a. The realist theatre holds a mirror up to life to celebrate its true joys and happiness.
    b. The realist theatre attempts to break through the limitation of language and character in order to arrive at an insight in a greater metaphysical cosmos.
    c. The realist theatre attempts to break away from the conventions and scenes of everyday life.
  * d. The realist theatre is a kind of laboratory in which the nature of relationships or the ills of society or the symptoms of the family can be set down for the final judgment of the audience.
    226

18. How was the proscenium stage of the romantic theatre modified to accommodate realist drama?
    a. The proscenium was dropped altogether to eliminate any division between the stage and the audience.
  * b. Box sets were made exactly to scale with full-dimension walls, real bookcases, windows, and fireplaces.
    c. Box sets were designed with special perspective lines to give the set the illusion of reality.
    d. The stage was physically raised and curtains were eliminated to reinforce the realist view that drama was "life on a pedestal."
    226

19. The "theatre of the fourth wall" refers to the central convention of realism, that is
  * a. the stage was conceived to be the same as life in a real-world setting, except that in the case of the stage one wall—the proscenium opening—had been removed.
    b. the human animal is seen to be like a rat in a maze, a creature bound by the strictures of walls, those walls being society, family, and economics.
    c. the fourth wall refers to the mind and the ability of the imagination to create a frame around the experience and thus complete an experience, just as a fourth wall completes a room.
    d. three walls are Marxist economics, Darwinian biological determinism, and Freudian psychological determinism.
    227

20. Which of the following is true of the realist view of character?
    a. Characters are defined by their symbolic names.
  * b. Characters are defined by true-to-life detail.
    c. Characters are defined by the ideologies or abstract idealizations that they voice.
    d. Characters are defined by their nationality and patriotic principles.
    227

21. The founding playwright of the realist era was
*   a.   Henrik Ibsen.
     b.   August Strindberg.
     c.   Mario Tinburgen.
     d.   Anton Chekov.
     227

22. The early plays of Ibsen treated
     a.   the role of democracy in the communist world.
*   b.   women's role in society, hereditary disease, and mercy killing.
     c.   environmental and animal rights.
     d.   the conflict with economics and authoritarianism in establishing a new world order.
     227

23. The problem in a "problem" play refers to
     a.   aesthetic problems: such plays created dramaturgical confusion from the standpoint of neoclassical aesthetics because they mixed social classes.
*   b.   the play's subject matter: a problem play is a realistic play that deals, narrowly, with a specific social problem.
     c.   a moral dilemma: a problem play portrays good and evil in strictly delimited ways to prevent moral ambiguity from creating a perceptual problem.
     d.   technical difficulty: problem plays were difficult to produce because they called for elaborate staging and machinery to create fires, automobile accidents, and airplane wrecks.
     227

24. Which of the following is NOT a realist dramatist correctly paired with his play?
     a.   George Bernard Shaw, *Mrs. Warren's Profession*
     b.   Gerhart Hauptmann, *The Weavers*
     c.   Eugène Brieux, *Damaged Goods*
*   d.   Antonin Artaud, *Jet of Blood*
     227, 230

25. Which of the following is true of the relationship between naturalism and realism?
     a.   "Naturalism" and "realism" are interchangeable terms.
*   b.   Naturalism is a philosophical concept concerning the nature of the human animal; "realism" refers to an artistic convention.
     c.   "Naturalism" is a word applied to the success of the performance; "realism" refers to the dramatic style.
     d.   "Naturalism" refers to a historical period that followed the age of realism.
     230

26. The high point of stylistic realism is best exemplified by
*   a.   Anton Chekhov.
     b.   August Strindberg.
     c.   Henrik Ibsen.
     d.   George Bernard Shaw.
     230

27. In plays including *The Sea Gull, The Three Sisters,* and *Uncle Vanya,* this playwright draws complex relationships among his characters and develops his plots and themes between the lines.
    a. George Bernard Shaw
  * b. Anton Chekhov
    c. August Strindberg
    d. Henrik Ibsen
    230–231

28. Chekhov wrote plays for which company?
    a. Veovold's World Palace Theatre
    b. Antoine's Théâtre Libre
    c. Syzslo's National Polish Theatre
  * d. Stanislavski's Moscow Art Theatre
    232

29. An unwilling spinster by accident of fate, this character from Chekhov's *The Three Sisters* is the leader, the family historian, the repository of confidences who holds the household on an even keel.
  * a. Olga
    b. Irina
    c. Masha
    d. Natalya
    234

30. In Chekhov's plays, the pauses (indicated by dashes), the repetitions, and the vagueness show
    a. the absence of intellectual commitment to ideas.
  * b. the rhythms and inanities of natural speech, which are contradicted by the characters' tone and actions.
    c. the absurdity of the universe in which language has no capacity to mean anything.
    d. the original problems in the handwritten playscript.
    235

31. What is the significance of the samovar that Tchebutykin presents to Irina for her birthday?
    a. A samovar was a typical wedding present, and he betrays his unconscious desires to marry Irina.
    b. A samovar was brought out only on the occasion of funerals, and Tchebutykin foreshadows his impending death.
  * c. A samovar was a silver anniversary present and more suited to Irina's mother, Tchebutykin's beloved, than to Irina.
    d. A silver samovar was an object permitted only to members of the royal family, and Tchebutykin betrays his class by this gift.
    235

32. How did Stanislavski contribute to realist theatre?
    * a. He brought realist acting to realist plots.
    b. He introduced body doubles in scenes of realistic passion.
    c. He introduced the use of complex nudity on the stage.
    d. He required actors and actresses to wear their own clothes on the stage.
    245

33. Masha and Vershinin's kiss in *The Three Sisters* shows
    a. how language substitutes for real passion.
    * b. how visceral and physiologically real their relationship was.
    c. how chastity can best symbolize a meeting of spirit and mind.
    d. how betrayal is best symbolized in the signs of its opposite.
    245

34. How do stage properties function in Chekhov's plays?
    a. Objects like the samovar show the realistic attributes of the living room and the bedroom.
    b. Objects are seen to be peripheral to the lives of the characters.
    * c. Action and character are conveyed *through* the objects.
    d. Objects become weapons and projectiles.
    245–246

35. The ending of Chekhov's *The Three Sisters*
    a. gives a moral about the need to remain faithful to one's spouse.
    b. shows the neat unwinding of an Aristotelian plot.
    * c. allows no firm conclusions to be drawn.
    d. shows that God is ever present as a benevolent force in the universe.
    246

36. Theatre activity in the United States can be dated from
    * a. the 1500s in Spanish.
    b. the 1500s in French.
    c. the tenth century in Native American dialects.
    d. the 1700s in English.
    246

37. America's first master dramatist was
    a. Lope de Vega.
    * b. Eugene O'Neill.
    c. Arthur Miller.
    d. Tennessee Williams.
    246

38. *Mourning Becomes Electra* is
* a. a rewriting of the Orestian trilogy in a puritanical New England setting, with Freudian motivation replacing Greek fates.
   b. a rewriting of Homer's *Odyssey,* with death being symbolized by economic and spiritual bankruptcy.
   c. a contemporary upbeat comedy that uses the mask of Electra as its central theme.
   d. a family romance in which characters and their Jungian archetypes act out stories from myth.
   247

39. Which of the following is NOT an American playwright?
   a. Robert Anderson
   b. William Gibson
   c. Lorraine Hansberry
* d. Tom Stoppard
   250

40. Which of the following is true of Chekhov's style?
* a. Chekhov suffuses his plays with gentle irony.
   b. Chekhov never uses irony in his plays.
   c. Chekhov builds on the device of the apostrophe: his plays always involve one character who is never present—who is either dead, exiled, or lost—as a significant element in his plays.
   d. Chekhov avoids elaborate realistic sets, preferring instead drawing room stages with few props.
   234

41. The eloquence of realistic drama may be seen in
* a. details of dialogue and action.
   b. cogent declamation.
   c. elaborate verse.
   d. blank verse spoken by the main characters.
   241

42. Chekhovian productions—and other realist works—were aided by the performance innovations introduced by
* a. Konstantin Stanislavski.
   b. André Meyerhold.
   c. Denis Diderot.
   d. Antonin Artaud.
   231

43. Which play by the American realist Arthur Miller deals with the broken dream of American success?
* a. *Death of a Salesman*
   b. *The Crucible*
   c. *A View from the Bridge*
   d. *After the Fall*
   249

44. Which of the following is NOT a play by Tennessee Williams?
    a. *Cat on a Hot Tin Roof*
    b. *The Glass Menagerie*
    c. *Suddenly Last Summer*
  * d. *All My Sons*
    250

45. Which of the following is NOT a favorite theme of realist drama?
    a. man's ignorance, failure, and isolation in an uncaring cosmos
    b. human confusion in a complicated world
  * c. nobility of love and striving
    d. human ignorance and failure
    226

46. Who was the chief theoretician of naturalism?
    a. Voltaire
    b. Sigmund Freud
  * c. Émile Zola
    d. Jack Deppe
    230

47. Which is the most widely known of all modern Russian plays?
  * a. *The Three Sisters*
    b. *Hedda Gabler*
    c. *Miss Julie*
    d. *Dr. Zhivago*
    232

48. Which contemporary dramatic form is superficially Chekhovian in structure?
    a. the full-length movie thriller
  * b. the soap opera
    c. the documentary
    d. the revival tragedy
    231

49. The subject matter of naturalistic plays was
    a. well-defined social issues.
    b. the conflict among nations.
  * c. slice-of-life drama.
    d. the symbolic expansion of ordinary events or objects.
    230

50. Which of the following is NOT a Chekhovian play?
  * a. *Miss Julie*
    b. *The Seagull*
    c. *Uncle Vanya*
    d. *The Cherry Orchard*
    230

ESSAY QUESTIONS

51. Compare and contrast Restoration and realist theatres in terms of their treatment of acting conventions, stage design, and subject matter.

52. Compare and contrast realist and naturalistic theatres. To what extent may naturalism be seen as an outgrowth of realism?

53. How did the contributions of Freud, Darwin, and Marx contribute to the realist theatre?

54. What contribution did romanticism make to the modern theatre in terms of character or theatre architecture?

55. Using O'Neill's *Mourning Becomes Electra* as your example, discuss the use of realism to expose psychological and mythic truth.

56. Using Chekhov's *The Three Sisters* as your example, discuss the function of the set (stage design and props) as an element that furthers character conflict. How are human relationships literally and metaphorically negotiated through properties?

57. Choose one character from Chekhov's *The Three Sisters* and analyze the language. How does the character's language reflect his or her situation in the play? Is irony a part of that characterization? How does it contribute to our understanding of the character?

58. Chekhov's drama is characterized by "laughing through tears." The happiest memories evoke the most painful realizations. The tension between the reality of the situation and the character's real feelings about his or her situation is one way that Chekhov uses irony; this use of irony in turn contributes to the way that Chekhov draws characters of great complexity. Discuss Chekhov's use of irony to create psychological depth in one or more characters from a play of your choice.

Chapter 9

The Modern Theatre: Antirealism

1. The antirealist movement in aesthetics had its roots in
* a. the symbolist movement in art.
   b. neoclassical aesthetics.
   c. the Fauve movement in painting.
   d. the biomechanical school of acting.
   251

2. The symbolist movement began as
   a. a reactionary political movement launched against social issues.
* b. an artistic movement of artists of every stripe, including playwrights, essayists, sculptors, and poets.
   c. a political reaction to realism grounded in the work of Spanish oil painters.
   d. an economic rebellion whose major spokespersons were those European sculptors who decried the high cost of materials.
   251

3. The first symbolist theatre
* a. was founded in 1890 by the Parisian poet Paul Fort.
   b. was founded in 1887 by André Antoine.
   c. was founded in 1926 by Antonin Artaud.
   d. was founded in 1896 by Alfred Jarry.
   252

4. Which events contributed to the advent of symbolism and the subsequent revolution of the stage?
* a. World War I and the growth of technology
   b. the rise of the Italian communist party and the consequent censorship of play texts
   c. the flourishing of a strong labor party in England and the subsequent emphasis on factory production
   d. World War II, which, through the drafting of men for war, created an audience composed primarily of working women with an income
   256

5. What two theatres emerged in the direct aftermath of World War II to dominate the Cold War era?
   a. theatre of cruelty and theatricalism
   b. symbolism and expressionism
* c. theatre of the absurd and theatre of alienation
   d. realist drama and social satire
   271

6. Which of the following playwrights did NOT experiment with both naturalist/realist and symbolist elements?
   a. Henrik Ibsen
   b. August Strindberg
 * c. Tom Stoppard
   d. Herbert Hauptmann
   253

7. Characters in symbolic drama were used to represent
   a. the conflict between man and nature or humanity and metaphysical forces in an ordered universe.
 * b. philosophical ideas or warring internal forces.
   c. true-to-life individuals.
   d. types and stereotypes in a return to Restoration aesthetics.
   251–252

8. Which of the following is true of symbolism?
 * a. Symbolism explored through images and metaphors the inner realities that cannot be directly or literally perceived.
   b. Symbolism exposed the social injustices of the working classes by means of irony.
   c. Symbolism tested the limits of language and decorum through the use of nonsense language and animal utterance.
   d. Symbolism uncovered the hidden subversive relationships in family histories by means of extended exposition.
   251

9. Which of the following is consistent with the symbolist opposition to realism?
   a. In order to subvert realism, symbolist writers attempted to draw characters more true to life than reality.
 * b. The symbolist spirit hated literal detail, the mundane, and the ordinary and therefore demanded abstraction and enlargement.
   c. In order to assault the dimensions of lived reality, symbolist drama fostered the use of miniature by plays-within-the-plays acted by puppets.
   d. In protest against realistic set and stage design, symbolist sets did away with all props and furniture on the stage.
   252

10. The theatre of the absurd was formulated by the existentialist writings of French essayist and playwright
    a. Jean Paul Sartre.
    b. Simone de Beauvoir.
    c. Alfred Jarry.
 * d. Albert Camus.
    271

11. Which of the following is true of the antirealist aesthetic?
    a. It fostered a return to character types, to rhymed language and mannered acting styles.
    * b. No restrictions were placed on the mixing of styles; thus, no absolute single set of governing principles determined the course of this theatre.
    c. Marinetti's concept of "convulsive beauty" led to the growth of a theatre without written play texts and in which actors did not know from one performance to the next which character they would play.
    d. It ironized realism by adopting the very same staging and acting conventions of realism.
    256

12. A stylized acting style is one in which
    * a. characters usually represent more than individual persons or personality types.
    b. characters do not transcend the limitations of their place but are instead shown as strict individuals in a laboratory setting.
    c. characters adopt set mannerisms and speech patterns taken from books on declamation and rhetoric.
    d. characters show only a select range of human responses in order to give the audience a "slice of life."
    256

13. This theatre attempted to alienate the audience by repudiating realistic conventions through a didactic performance style, an acting style that required the actor to "demonstrate" rather than integrate with his character, and a stage that called attention to its own artificiality.
    * a. Brecht's theatre of alienation
    b. Artaud's theatre of cruelty
    c. Pirandello's theatricalism
    d. Beckett's realism
    288

14. The alienation effect was intended to
    a. enhance the audience's engagement with the characters.
    b. foster the audience's belief in the dramatic illusion.
    * c. prevent the audience's engagement with the magic of theatre.
    d. force the audience to recognize social evil as it saw scenes of drama which antagonized it.
    288

15. In this play, a good-hearted prostitute receives a gift of money from three itinerant gods and uses the money to start a tobacco business.
    a. Shaw's *Man and Superman*
    b. O'Neill's *Mourning Becomes Electra*
    * c. Brecht's *Good Woman of Sezuan*
    d. Beckett's *Happy Days*
    288

16. Which of the following plays was NOT a symbolist play?
    a. Hauptmann's *The Sunken Bell*
    b. Jarry's *Ubu Roi*
*   c. Beckett's *Happy Days*
    d. Barrie's *Peter Pan*
    253

17. When symbolism as a movement was deserted by founders and followers, it found form in other movements. Which of the following did NOT emerge as an extension of the symbolist movement?
    a. idealism
    b. impressionism
*   c. naturalism
    d. Dada
    255

18. Which period of drama produced a flourishing of manifestos?
    a. realist
*   b. symbolist
    c. naturalist
    d. impressionist
    256

19. Which of the following is NOT a typical theme of the symbolist theatre?
    a. the intransigence of despair
    b. the futility of communication
    c. the loss of innocence
*   d. the failure of commonwealths
    257

20. In this absurdist drama, a woman partially buried alive in a mound of earth awaits her destiny.
    a. Sartre's *No Exit*
    b. Artaud's *Jet of Blood*
    c. Beckett's *Endgame*
*   d. Beckett's *Happy Days*
    275

21. The theatre of the absurd adopts as its emblem the sufferings of the mythological Greek
    a. Prometheus.
    b. Oedipus.
*   c. Sisyphus.
    d. Cassandra.
    271

22. "Avant-garde" means
*   a. literally, "the major assault" or "shock troops."
    b. "historically coming before."
    c. "up on your guard"—in other words, "get ready."
    d. "after the old ones die."
    257

23. *Coup de théâtre* refers to
    a. a character being murdered onstage.
    * b. an event unpredicted by anything in the play up to that point and yet wholly consistent with what has gone on before.
    c. a political theme in which a leader is deposed.
    d. a type of stage chair that can be lowered or raised at will.
    282

24. *Verfremdung* is a German word meaning
    a. absurdity.
    * b. alienation or distancing.
    c. dramatic irony.
    d. existential dilemma.
    286

25. Ibsen had tested the boundaries of subject matter in his plays. Who tested the Victorian language barriers by using obscenities and vulgar epithets?
    a. Shaw
    * b. Jarry
    c. Shepherd
    d. Stoppard
    257

26. "Surrealism," meaning
    * a. "super realism," was coined by André Breton.
    b. "above realism," was coined by the painter Vasquez.
    c. "beyond realism," was coined by Picasso.
    d. "un-real," was coined by Antonin Artaud.
    259

27. In this play, four characters who are the seeming survivors of a nuclear holocaust live out their last days in a surrealistic landscape where there is no painkiller to assuage their moral and physical agony.
    * a. Beckett's *Endgame*
    b. Pirandello's *Six Characters in Search of an Author*
    c. Sartre's *No Exit*
    d. Beckett's *Happy Days*
    275

28. This type of drama, in vogue in Germany during the first two decades of the century, featured shocking dialogue, boldly exaggerated scenery, piercing sounds, bright lights, an abundance of primary colors, a not very subtle use of symbols, and a structure of short, stark, jabbing scenes building to a powerful or deafening climax.
    a. impressionism
    b. theatre of cruelty
    * c. expressionism
    d. Dada
    262

29. Which type of drama meets the following description? The theatre becomes a part of the content of play production, not merely the vehicle.
    a. impressionism
*   b. theatricalism
    c. expressionism
    d. theatre of cruelty
    265

30. An example of a type of play in which theatre becomes a theme rather than simply the vehicle is
    a. *The Hairy Ape.*
*   b. *Six Characters in Search of an Author.*
    c. *Death of A Salesman.*
    d. *Prometheus Unbound.*
    265

31. In *Six Characters in Search of an Author,* Pirandello uses the theme of the theatricality of human existence to show
*   a. that everyday life is beset by the eternal confusion between appearance and reality.
    b. that appearances, while deceiving, can be grounded in an ultimate reality.
    c. the ultimate authority of truth to establish the difference between appearance and reality.
    d. that appearance is ephemeral and easy to dismiss.
    266

32. The philosophy that every individual seeks affirmation and self-realization in the eyes of the Other but fails to find certification of final personal worth is consistent with
    a. Strindberg's view of expressionism.
    b. the role of the unconscious in Ibsen.
*   c. Sartre's existentialism.
    d. Dali's surrealism.
    269

33. Which of the following most accurately explains the difference between expressionism and existentialism?
*   a. Expressionism and existentialism are radically different: the former denotes an artistic style growing from the influence of psychoanalysis and consequent emphasis on the unconscious, whereas the latter is a philosophy of being that uses drama to articulate its themes.
    b. Expressionism and existentialism are very close in philosophical concept: expressionism maintains that each individual has the right to express himself or herself; existentialism holds that the right of self-expression is inherent in the human existence.
    c. These terms denote different ideas. Expressionism was only an artistic movement in the visual arts; existentialism was an artistic movement related to the symbolist movement in Paris in the twenties and has no bearing on drama.
    d. The difference between expressionism and existentialism is primarily geographical: both expressionism and existentialism were offshoots of the constructivist movement, but expressionism found its clearest vocalizations in England, whereas existentialism found its clearest manifestation in France.
    270

34. Which of the following is true of characterization in Sartre's *No Exit?*
* a. The characters represent philosophical rather than psychological wholes.
   b. The characters represent the essential bifurcation of the human condition into appearance and reality.
   c. The characters represent psychologically unified beings rather than types.
   d. The characters represent the role of the unconscious when it is forced into action in social situations.
   270

35. George Bernard Shaw's legacy of a witty, unsentimental, and fiercely intelligent verbal style has extended to
* a. Simon Gray, Alan Ayckbourne, and Tom Stoppard.
   b. Roger Blin, Peter Brook, and Jerzy Kosinski.
   c. Eugène Ionesco, Edward Albee, and Harold Pinter.
   d. Arthur Miller and Eugene O'Neill.
   262

36. Among those who inherited Artaud's dramatic legacy are
   a. Alan Ayckbourne and Simon Gray.
   b. Peter Shaffer and Eugene O'Neill.
* c. Peter Brook and Jerzy Grotowski.
   d. Eugène Ionesco and Harold Pinter.
   269

37. Which of the following playwrights did NOT write in the tradition of the theatre of the absurd?
   a. Jean Genet
   b. Eugène Ionesco
   c. Edward Albee
* d. Arthur Miller
   273

38. A great theorist of the drama, this person founded the Theatre Alfred Jarry in 1926, produced Strindberg's *Dream Play* and adapted Shelley's *The Cenci,* and theorized a theatre of cruelty that was more significant for its ideas than for the actual plays it produced:
   a. George Bernard Shaw
   b. Luigi Pirandello
* c. Antonin Artaud
   d. Alfred Jarry
   267

39. The constructivist who broke with Stanislavski's style of realist performance to create a nonrealist "biomechanical" style of acting and direction was
   a. François Medvedev.
   b. Mikhail Bakhtin.
* c. Vsevolod Meyerhold.
   d. Bertolt Brecht.
   254

40. Who said, "Art has nothing to do with clarity, does not dabble in the clear, and does not make clear"?
   a. George Bernard Shaw
 * b. Samuel Beckett
   c. Antonin Artaud
   d. Eugène Ionesco
   273

41. In Beckett's play *Happy Days,* Brownie is the name of
   a. the female protagonist.
   b. the male protagonist.
   c. the location.
 * d. the revolver.
   282

42. The foremost American playwright whose ventures into naturalism eventually turned toward expressionism and the authorship of *The Hairy Ape* was
   a. Ernest Hemingway.
 * b. Eugene O'Neill.
   c. Alan Ayckbourne.
   d. Simon Gray.
   262

43. This playwright was born in Dublin in 1906 and emigrated to Paris in 1928. His career was marked by artistic vagabondage, during which time he wrote several short stories and poems. During the Occupation in the south of France he wrote masterworks for which he is famous, among which stands the play *Waiting for Godot.*
   a. James Joyce
 * b. Samuel Beckett
   c. Eugene O'Neill
   d. John Millington Synge
   273–274

44. The slogan of "No more masterpieces" characterizes
   a. Stanislavski's school of realism.
 * b. Artaud's theatre of cruelty.
   c. Pirandello's theatricalism.
   d. Brecht's epic theatre.
   267

45. In this play, written by a well-known French existentialist, hell is a room without windows or mirrors where ill-matched characters confront an infinite bleakness; hell is other people.
   a. Artaud's *Jet of Blood*
   b. Pirandello's *Six Characters in Search of an Author*
 * c. Sartre's *No Exit*
   d. Shaw's *Major Barbara*
   269

46. This producer and critic made the distinction between "holy" and "rough" theatres.
    a. Peter Schaffer
  * b. Peter Brook
    c. Alan Ayckbourne
    d. Bertolt Brecht
    290

47. This playwright, born in Germany in 1898, emerged from World War I as a dedicated Marxist and pacifist and consolidated his theories about drama into a body of plays that include *The Rise and Fall of the City of Mahagonny*.
    a. Antonin Artaud
    b. Konstantin Stanislavski
    c. Herbert Hauptmann
  * d. Bertolt Brecht
    287

48. Which playwright, famous for his wit, used the stage as a vehicle for ideas?
  * a. George Bernard Shaw
    b. Bertolt Brecht
    c. Luigi Pirandello
    d. Tom Stoppard
    260

49. This play is a savage and often ludicrous satire on the theme of power; in it, a fat, foul-mouthed father is the driving force for farce and violence.
    a. Artaud's *Jet of Blood*
    b. Beckett's *Endgame*
  * c. Jarry's *Ubu Roi*
    d. Pirandello's *Six Characters in Search of an Author*
    258

50. Which production had the most violent opening in theatre history, such that the audience shouted, hissed, threw things, and fought duels after subsequent performances?
  * a. Jarry's *Ubu Roi*
    b. Brecht's *Mother Courage*
    c. Artaud's *Conquest of Mexico*
    d. Shaw's *Major Barbara*
    257

51. This playwright and dramatist provided a new kind of dramaturgy that intended a wholesale repudiation of Aristotelian catharsis (which depends on the audience's empathy) and a denial of Stanislavski's basic principles concerning the aims of the acting.
    a. Antonin Artaud
  * b. Bertolt Brecht
    c. Vsevolod Meyerhold
    d. Eugene O'Neill
    288

52. This play, a parable without a message, reveals a paradigm of human condition in which characters exchange songs, give accounts of dreams, and try to make the best of a hopeless situation.
    a. Sartre's *No Exit*
 * b. Beckett's *Waiting for Godot*
    c. Jarry's *Ubu Roi*
    d. Maeterlinck's *The Intruder*
    275

ESSAY QUESTIONS

53. Explain how *The Hairy Ape* shows expressionist principles.

54. Because irony is based on a discrepancy (between a character's thoughts and acts; between a character's view of himself and others' views of him; between the real and ideal; between what should be and what is—to name only a few kinds of discrepancy), it has traditionally been seen as a trope that turns against (criticizes or exposes) something. Begin with a definition of irony that focuses on one type of discrepancy and then elaborate that definition through one of Shaw's plays.

55. Discuss the role of the set in producing expressionist effects in O'Neill's *The Hairy Ape*.

56. Discuss the role of the past in Ibsen.

57. Using *The Hairy Ape* as your example, discuss the way that O'Neill used realism and romanticism in his representation of social ideology and cultural criticism.

58. In one of his manifestos, Artaud said that theatre should "cut through language and touch life." How did Artaud view language? scripts? Analyze Artaud's view of the limits of language. Explain how Artaud's theoretical view—that theatre was a force that could transcend language—could be worked out in practical ways in an actual production. Take a traditional play that you have already studied—Aeschylus' *Prometheus Bound* would make an effective choice—and explain how it could be staged in the theatre of cruelty.

59. Discuss the difference between expressionism and impressionism using two plays of your choice as examples.

60. Compare and contrast *Prometheus Bound* with *Happy Days* in terms of the way that the characters' containment by the set is central to the subsequent unfolding of the play.

61. How did World War I influence the antirealist theatre?

62. Explain the distinction between "holy" and "rough" theatres. If, as Peter Brook maintains, Beckett and Brecht represent these two poles, how would O'Neill fit into the continuum marked by Beckett at the "holy" end and Brecht at the "rough" end? How would Artaud (Jarry, Shaw) fit in?

63. Discuss and explain the innovations Brecht brought to acting and staging conventions.

Chapter 10 / Brief: Chapter 8
Theatre Today

 1. The theatre may be considered a conservative institution because it conserves or preserves
    a.   a consistent ideology characteristic of political parties.
*   b.   the history and conventional way of working as a theatre.
    c.   the political and economic views of the time.
    d.   the moral attitudes of a select group of people.
    292
    Brief: 228

2. All of the following happened reflecting the collapse in the postmodern social order by an extremity in artistic representation EXCEPT
    a.   legal censorship became locally unenforceable in America.
    b.   play-licensing laws in England fell.
    c.   open copulation, bold profanity, and total nudity were shown onstage.
*   d.   the actual death of Death Row prisoners was enacted on the stage.
    292
    Brief: 228

3. The crisis in representation that led to postmodern aesthetics was caused by all of the following EXCEPT
    a.   the resignation of a sitting president and vice president in the United States.
    b.   the civilized world's recognition of past and present horrors, from the Holocaust to the vast destruction of world natural resources.
    c.   the prospering of crime and terrorism as empires began to crumble.
*   d.   the renewed intellectual life in the academy, which influenced art in theory and practice.
    292
    Brief: 228

 4. The age of license and unrestricted dramaturgical violence came to an end
*   a.   by the late 1970s.
    b.   by the end of the 1960s.
    c.   by the beginning of the 1980s.
    d.   by the beginning of the 1990s.
    293
    Brief: 229

 5. Postmodern theatre is characterized by all of the following EXCEPT
    a.   a theatre of revival.
    b.   a theatre of experiment.
    c.   an open theatre.
*   d.   a theatre of stereotypes.
    293
    Brief: 229

6. A general desire for the sublime harmonies created by artists of another age, prompted by the excesses of the sixties and the anarchic violence of late modernist art, may account for the swell in
   a. postmodern experimentation.
 * b. revival theatre.
   c. melodrama.
   d. "boulevard theatre."
   294
   Brief: 230

7. All of the following statements exemplify the postmodern trend toward revival EXCEPT
   a. Seventy-eight theatre companies in almost every state in America are devoted to producing Shakespearean festivals.
   b. Elaborate stagings of nineteenth-century novels signal the revival of romantic elements.
   c. The restaging of American musicals from the golden era of the 1940s, 50s, and 60s accounts for one-half to two-thirds of the offerings on Broadway.
 * d. Plays that dramatize the life of the ancient playwrights account for a quarter of the productions off-Broadway.
   294
   Brief: 230

8. Which of the following is NOT true of postmodernism?
 * a. Postmodernism values logic and cause-effect determinism.
   b. Postmodernism emphasizes self-reflection and reflections on the past.
   c. Postmodernism emphasizes the artist's redefining a commercial product as an independent work of art.
   d. Postmodernism makes some kind of statement about art.
   295
   Brief: 231

9. How do postmodern aesthetics relate to previous aesthetics?
   a. Postmodern theatre lacks the modernist's social or aesthetic optimism.
   b. Postmodern theatre sees the symbolist and surrealist attempt to reveal a higher truth as unreachable.
   c. Since social progress is unattainable according to postmodern ideology, the artist is wary of the future.
 * d. Postmodern theatre attempts to illuminate the received truths of realism.
   296
   Brief: 232

10. The *métaphore manquée* refers to
   a. the self-defining metaphor.
 * b. the missing metaphor.
   c. the overruling metaphor that defines everything in terms of itself.
   d. the metaphor of French culture.
   296
   Brief: 232

11. Which of the following is NOT a postmodern art form?
    a. the action painting of Jackson Pollock
    b. breakdancing
    c. the music of John Cage
 * d. the concerts of Christopher Hogwood's School of Ancient Music
    297
    Brief: 233

12. The roots of postmodern theatre can be located in the arts phenomenon called
    a. surrealism.
 * b. Dadaism.
    c. expressionism.
    d. symbolism.
    297
    Brief: 233

13. Begun in 1916 in Zurich, Switzerland, this art movement was characterized by a mix of singing, recitations, paintings, chance poetry, and a general chaos emblematized by the poetry of Tristan Tzara.
    a. surrealism
    b. expressionism
 * c. Dada
    d. postmodernism
    297
    Brief: 233

14. This theatre, with a brilliant innovative company formed by Joseph Chaikin in 1963, combined social improvisation with Brechtian techniques and used character as a vehicle for direct interaction with audiences; it was known as
 * a. The Open Theatre.
    b. The Teatro Campesino.
    c. New Lafayette Theatre.
    d. The Women's Collective.
    298
    Brief: 234

15. Which of the following is NOT true of the role of women in the history of drama?
    a. Until the seventeenth century, women were virtually unrepresented in the theatre.
    b. Until the 1950s, women were largely relegated to acting and to costume construction.
    c. One-third of the 200+ regional theatres are now headed by women.
 * d. Women have never been so underrepresented in drama as directors and producers since the 1650s.
    298–299
    Brief: 234–235

16. Founded by Luis Valdez in 1965, which contemporary Chicano theatre was created to dramatize the farmworkers' situation in California through *actos?*
    a. Carmina Burana
  * b. Teatro Campesino
    c. Teatro Milagro
    d. Teatro la Raza
    302
    Brief: 238

17. What is the name of the first play staged in the United States, at the San Juan Pueblo outside of Santa Fe (then Mexico)?
  * a. *Los moros y los cristianos*
    b. *La noche de la vida*
    c. *Sol y sombre*
    d. *Tambien El Capitan*
    302
    Brief: 238

18. The author of *M. Butterfly,* a play that reinterprets the Madame Butterfly story, mixing up racial stereotypes and gender stereotypes, and that incorporates Peking Opera technique with Western drama, is
    a. Maxine Hong Kingston.
    b. Amy Tan.
  * c. David Henry Hwang.
    d. Li Y'iang.
    304
    Brief: 240

19. A *zarzuela* is
  * a. a light operetta.
    b. a melodramatic soap opera.
    c. a form of farce involving women.
    d. a politically sensitive vignette taken from a novel.
    302
    Brief: 238

20. The playwright and theorist who combined prehistoric performance techniques drawn from around the world to create an objective drama that sought to dissolve the unconsciously applied linguistic and cultural codes that separated human beings from their true biological and spiritual selves is
    a. David Henry Hwang.
    b. Peter Brook.
  * c. Jerzy Grotowski.
    d. Lorraine Hansberry.
    304
    Brief: 240

21. The representation of homosexuality
    a. was legal but repressed in England as late as 1960.
    * b. was illegal in England as late as 1958.
    c. was openly encouraged in the American theatre.
    d. was never illegal in England or America.
    305
    Brief: 241

22. "Nontraditional casting" means that
    a. actors are chosen for parts solely on the basis of their academic preparation.
    b. actors are chosen for parts on the basis of their ability to match the ethnicity and gender of the roles.
    * c. actors are chosen for parts based on criteria other than the physical matching of types to the roles.
    d. actors are chosen for parts through the intervention of intermediaries other than agents.
    306
    Brief: 242

23. The theatrical capital of the United States is
    a. Hollywood, California.
    b. Washington, D.C.
    c. Orlando, Florida.
    * d. New York City.
    308
    Brief: 244

24. Broadway is famous for all of the following EXCEPT
    a. the possibility of making it rich.
    b. the origin of spectacular musicals and the occasional new comedy or comedy review.
    * c. the origin of the most avant-garde intellectual drama and innovative dramaturgy.
    d. America's premier commercial theater.
    309
    Brief: 245

25. "The Great White Way" refers to
    a. off-Broadway.
    * b. Broadway.
    c. the Village.
    d. SoHo.
    309
    Brief: 245

26. Professional theatres found primarily in Greenwich Village, SoHo, and the upper East and West sides of Manhattan and operating on siginificantly reduced budgets are collectively known as
    a. Broadway.
    * b. off-Broadway.
    c. off-off-Broadway.
    d. The Great White Way.
    313
    Brief: 249

27. Which of the following is NOT true of the difference between Broadway and its "off" variants?
    a. Off-Broadway activity is less costly than Broadway productions.
    b. Off-Broadway productions generally attract a specialized cadre of devotees.
    c. The most creative work done in American theatre has occurred in off-Broadway productions.
  * d. The least innovative dramaturgy has been seen in off-Broadway productions.
    313
    Brief: 249

28. Which of the following is NOT true of nonprofit theatres?
    a. "Nonprofit" means strictly "noncommercial," so that nonprofit theatres rely upon funding sources other than box office receipts.
    b. "Nonprofit" is strictly a legal designation: the theatre has no owners and makes no profit.
  * c. "Nonprofit" means that no one makes a profit; therefore, actors, stage designers, and all members involved in the production receive no salaries.
    d. Nonprofit theatres are exempt from most taxes.
    314
    Brief: 250

29. A variety of drama that originated in theatres once located in resort areas and that provided summer entertainment for tourists is known as
    a. off-off-Broadway.
  * b. summer stock.
    c. regional theatre.
    d. improv.
    320
    Brief: 256

30. This variety of theatre, broadly introduced to suburban Americans in the 1970s and producing light comedies and mystery melodramas and offering a night on the town, is commonly known as
    a. summer stock.
    b. off-Broadway.
  * c. dinner theater.
    d. comedy club.
    322
    Brief: 258

31. The most significant difference between contemporary European theatre and American theatre is that
  * a. the European theatre is highly institutionalized, with state-supported and city-supported theatres.
    b. the European theatre is closer to the intellectual and philosophical tradition of the classics.
    c. the European theatre is the more innovative, by way of new technology.
    d. the European theatre has made a stronger link between drama and filmmaking.
    324
    Brief: 260

32. Which of the following is NOT true of the relationship between the theatre and the academy?
   a. Stage performances have been used in schools since the Renaissance to teach dramatic literature, foreign language, and presentation skills.
   b. Academic and professional theatres have grown progressively closer, with an interchange of actors and artists.
   c. Long before the development of nonprofit professional theatre, universities and colleges were providing audiences around the country with masterworks of the international dramatic repertory.
 * d. The academy and the theatre have had a long history of opposition since the rise of medieval monasticism.
   324–325
   Brief: 260–261

 33. Shakespeare festivals, which began in 1935 and are now held in every state in the nation, originated with
 * a. summer stock productions.
   b. off-Broadway productions.
   c. an offshoot of Broadway productions.
   d. the influence of English writers in America.
   329
   Brief: 265

34. "Boulevard theatre" in France refers to
   a. a melodrama involving bankruptcy.
 * b. a light diverting piece on the theme of marital infidelity.
   c. performance art pieces played out in cafes.
   d. a soap opera concerned with Mafia intrigue.
   327
   Brief: 263

 35. Which of the following is true of performance art?
   a. Performance art recognizes the conventions of drama.
 * b. Performance art creates a series of visual happenings and audial rhythms often interwoven with some sort of spoken narratives or dialogues.
   c. There is a clear plot in performance art.
   d. The performers act in character, not as themselves.
   327
   Brief: 263

 36. Which Western country may be credited with the most radical innovations in the area of directing and design?
   a. the United States
   b. France
 * c. Germany
   d. England
   329
   Brief: 265

37. Which dissident playwright was elected president?
    a. Václav Havel in Czechoslovakia
    b. Bill Clinton in America
    c. François Mitterand in France
    d. Brian Mulrooney in Canada
    330
    Brief: 266

38. Which South African playwright lodged a confrontation with apartheid in such plays as *Sizwe Banzai Is Dead, The Island,* and *Master Harold and the Boys?*
    * a. Athol Fugard
    b. Wole Soylinka
    c. Ainwande Oluwole
    d. Chinua Achebe
    330
    Brief: 266

39. This Japanese theatre form, influenced by modern European realism, spurred an avant-garde nonrealistic countermovement that is explosive, violent, sexual, acrobatic, and even sado-masochistic.
    a. Nō
    b. Kabuki
    * c. *shingeki*
    d. Bunraku
    331
    Brief: 267

40. A veteran of the Pilobolus dance troupe, which artist created two notable dance pieces in the late 1980s (*The Garden of Earthly Delights* and *Vienna Lusthaus*) that combined drama and ballet and that showed the influences of surrealism and Antonin Artaud?
    * a. Martha Clarke
    b. Martha Graham
    c. Maya Patterson
    d. Maya Angelou
    332
    Brief: 268

41. Which of the following is NOT a one-person show, i.e., a full-length play employing a single actor?
    * a. Andrew Lloyd Weber's *Phantom of the Opera*
    b. Chekhov's *On the Harmfulness of Tobacco*
    c. Patrick Stewart's presentation of Dickens's *A Christmas Carol*
    d. Jane Wagner's *The Search for Signs of Intelligent Life in the Universe*
    333
    Brief: 269

42. Ariane Mnouchkine's notion of collaborative creation includes all of the following EXCEPT
    *   a.   all the company members live in the same house.
        b.   productions grow from improvisations.
        c.   all members of the group share the responsibility of scriptwriting, staging, interpretation, design, and set construction.
        d.   all the company members receive the same salary.
    335
    Brief: 271

43. Now located in a former munitions factory, the Cartoucherie, in the Paris suburb of Vincennes, this theatre company sought a new language of theatre based on Artaudian freedom, Brechtian commitment, collective improvisation, and the blending of Eastern and Western performance traditions to stage productions based on plays linked by time, theme, and methodology.
        a.   Grotowski's Objective Theatre
        b.   Antoine's Théâtre Libre
        c.   Artaud's theatre of cruelty
    *   d.   Mnouchkine's Théâtre de Soleil
    336
    Brief: 272

44. *Tableaux vivants* refers to
        a.   poems that are sung or chanted.
        b.   a collection of characters.
    *   c.   a human assemblage that makes a living picture.
        d.   plays in which songs are performed at the beginning and end.
    337
    Brief: 273

45. A performance and theatre artist, which Texas-born artist came to prominence in Germany, received attention from the avant-garde for his *tableaux vivants,* and was invited to create the central performance work of the 1984 Los Angeles Olympic Arts Festival, *The CIVIL warS?*
    *   a.   Robert Wilson
        b.   Richard Foreman
        c.   Frank Butler
        d.   André Fort
    337
    Brief: 273

46. Which artist (b. 1930), credited with changing the face of American musicals, made his first mark with the composition of lyrics for Leonard Bernstein's *West Side Story?* He has gone on to produce controversial new works, among them a musical review called *Assassins,* which engages political assassination involving protagonists such as John Wilkes Booth, Lee Harvey Oswald, Squeaky Fromme, and John Hinckley.

*   a.   Stephen Sondheim
    b.   Graham Wilson
    c.   Peter Brook
    d.   Peter Shaffer
    339
    Brief: 275

 47. The most provocative director of the twentieth century (b. 1925), which English boy-wonder was famous for innovative direction of plays by Shakespeare, Marlowe, Cocteau, and Sartre? In 1971 he moved to Paris to create The International Center of Theatre Research; the publication of *The Empty Space* (1968), in which he divided modern drama into "the deadly theatre, the holy theatre, and the rough theatre," established his reputation as a theorist.

*   a.   Peter Brook
    b.   Langston Hughes
    c.   Graham Wilson
    d.   Andrew Lloyd Weber
    341–342
    Brief: 277–278

 48. Who was the leading American playwright (b. 1945) of the late 1980s and early 1990s, whose work includes *Ma Rainey's Black Bottom, Fences,* and *The Piano Lesson*—a canon of new plays that creates a decade-by-decade history of the lives and accomplishments of ordinary twentieth-century African Americans, presenting a lively and evocative description of black homelife within the context of white political society?

*   a.   August Wilson
    b.   Langston Hughes
    c.   Amiri Baraka
    d.   Lorraine Hansberry
    343
    Brief: 279

 49. Considered America's greatest playwright, which playwright (b. 1915) produced three plays in the 1990s that conflated twentieth-century social and medical themes, reflecting his continuing exploration and critique of the American body politic? His play *The Ride Down Mount Morgan* (which premiered in England in 1991) managed to bring in the warring generations, pleasure, guilt, marriage, money, children, race, sex, death, and business among its timely topics.

*   a.   Arthur Miller
    b.   Stephen Sondheim
    c.   Edward Albee
    d.   Lanford Wilson
    345
    Brief: 281

50. Winner of three Pulitzer Prizes, which playwright (b. 1928) is famous for *The Zoo Story, Who's Afraid of Virginia Woolf?* and *Krapp's Last Tape?*
   a.   August Wilson
   b.   Arthur Miller
   c.   Wendy Wasserstein
 * d.   Edward Albee
   347
   Brief: 283

51. A pioneer playwright in the heyday of New York's experimental theatre in the 1960s (b. 1937), his first plays, produced at the Café La Mama and Caffe Cino theatre bars, included evocative studies of male homosexuality (*The Madness of Lady Bright*), interracial marriage (*The Gingham Dog*), and small-town small-mindedness (*The Rimers of Eldritch*); he helped create the Circle Repertory Theatre in New York, which produced his celebrated *Hot L Baltimore.*
   a.   John Guare
 * b.   Lanford Wilson
   c.   David Mamet
   d.   Sam Shepard
   347
   Brief: 283

52. Born in 1938, which Yale graduate became widely known in New York with a series of surrealistic and "wacky" plays such as *Muzeeka* (1968) and *The House of Blue Leaves* (1970)? He burst onto the national scene with *Six Degrees of Separation,* which explores and acidly reveals racial stereotyping, contemporary parenting and misparenting, and the cultural dissonances in contemporary adult America.
   a.   Tony Kushner
   b.   David Henry Hwang
 * c.   John Guare
   d.   Sam Shepard
   348
   Brief: 284

53. Although his first play, . . . *And Things That Go Into the Night* (1965), was virtually booed off the stage, giving this playwright a reputation as a raging young avant-gardist, the success of *The Kiss of the Spider Woman* earned which playwright (b. 1939) a Tony Award?
   a.   Arthur Miller
 * b.   Terence McNally
   c.   David Mamet
   d.   George C. Wolfe
   348
   Brief: 284

99

54. Born in 1943, which playwright received great acclaim in the 1970s and 80s with his *The Tooth of Crime, The Curse of the Starving Class, Buried Child* (awarded the Pulitzer Prize), *True West, Fool for Love,* and *A Lie of the Mind?* His plays are prose poems with highly musical language; more myth than reality, his plays invariably involve some violence to tantalize the audience with moments of extreme surface realism that ultimately opens on something more abstract.

*   a.   Sam Shepard
      b.   Stephen Sondheim
      c.   Terence McNally
      d.   August Wilson
348–349
Brief: 284–285

 55. Known as a Chicago playwright by birthplace, home, and the setting of his plays, and the artistic director of Chicago's Goodman Theatre, which playwright's plays employ fragments of intensely realistic dialogue, with characters' talk a series of frustrated stammerings, grunts, curses, repetitions, and trail-offs? Among his works are *American Buffalo* and *Glengarry Glen Ross.*

      a.   John Guare
      b.   Lanford Wilson
      c.   Terence McNally
*   d.   David Mamet
349
Brief: 285

 56. National attention focused on which playwright (b. 1947), whose first production was *Getting Out,* a driving, biting study of a woman's release from prison and her subsequent "imprisonment" by the forces of economics, male chauvinism, and sexual harassment? Her next play, *'night, Mother,* brutally depicted a sad young woman's suicide and her mother's inability to stop it.

      a.   Wendy Wasserstein
*   b.   Marsha Norman
      c.   Marsha Graham
      d.   Beth Henley
349
Brief: 285

 57. Which playwright (b. 1950), a graduate of Mount Holyoke and City College of New York, was highly admired for her successful off-Broadway play *Isn't It Romantic?* and whose work *The Heidi Chronicles* was created in workshop format at the Seattle Repertory Theatre before it opened on Broadway and captured both the Tony Award and the Pulitzer Prize in 1989?

      a.   Marsha Norman
      b.   Beth Henley
      c.   Aphra Behn
*   d.   Wendy Wasserstein
349
Brief: 285

58. Which playwright (b. 1952) was awarded the Pulitzer Prize in drama in 1981 for her *Crimes of the Heart,* a wildly irreverent comedy about three young Mississippi sisters coming together at joint crises in their lives? The play, while directly feminist in its themes, was one of the first major mainstream American plays to focus primarily on women's problems and women's issues.

* a. Beth Henley
  b. Wendy Wasserstein
  c. Marsha Norman
  d. Marsha Graham

351
Brief: 287

59. A Kentucky-born African American (1954), this playwright uses humor and music as wedges to explore deeply painful subjects. He skewers hoary clichés and persistent stereotypes of the "colored" world that emanate from both white and African-American subgroups. With *Jelly's Last Jam,* in 1992, a Broadway musical about the African-American jazz musician Jelly Roll Morton, this playwright went mainstream, winning Tony nominations for writing and directing.

  a. Tony Kushner
* b. George C. Wolfe
  c. John Guare
  d. Lanford Wilson

351
Brief: 287

60. Which New York–born, Louisiana-grown playwright (b. 1956) wrote a masterpiece of modern drama, *Angels in America,* considered the finest American play of the present generation? (It deals unstintingly with the AIDS crisis while it also lays bare unsettled issues that touch upon race, religion, politics, economics, and sexual orientation.)

  a. George C. Wolfe
  b. Stephen Sondheim
  c. David Henry Hwang
* d. Tony Kushner

352
Brief: 288

ESSAY QUESTIONS

61. The emphasis on multiculturalism and the changing state of global politics have broken the theatre away from many artistic conventions. Discuss the relationship between historical change and theatrical change. Make sure you focus your topic in such a way as to give it a depth of discussion.

62. As a research project, write a paper in which you characterize the theatre in your area. Make a survey of local commercial and academic theatres, and consider as well local performance artists. Can you identify any new forms or new kinds of art being generated in your area?

63. Diversity seems to be not only a political movement but also an important aesthetic one. Discuss the connection between politics and aesthetics in the postmodern world. You may, if you choose, reference your response with respect to earlier dramatic forms. (Can you think of an instance when aesthetics and politics were NOT intertwined? Could this interconnection account for the inherently conservative orientation of drama?)

64. Discuss the influence of Brecht, Artaud, and Dada on the aesthetics of postmodern theatre.

65. Ariane Mnouchkine's work in the Théâtre de Soleil shows the range of revival in drama. Discuss her work in the context of other kinds of revivals or revisions. What is the significance of the content of her plays? Her dramaturgical technique?

Chapter 11 / Brief: Chapter 3
The Actor

1. "Thespian" means
   * a.   actor.
   b.   the person in costume.
   c.   falsifier.
   d.   the person with a declamatory voice.
   360
   Brief: 62

2. "Mimesis" means
   a.   agitation.
   b.   falsification.
   c.   dissimulation.
   * d.   imitation.
   360
   Brief: 62

3. A person's earliest contact with mimesis comes through
   a.   a religious experience through ritual.
   * b.   the child's play, which explores adult roles.
   c.   a child's first contact with rules or laws.
   d.   an individual's first contact with instructions.
   360
   Brief: 62

4. What two kinds of imitation are necessary in acting?
   * a.   external mimesis and embodiment
   b.   embodiment and self-possession
   c.   external mimesis and self-reflection
   d.   embodiment and self-reflection
   360
   Brief: 62

5. Which of the following is NOT an example of external mimesis?
   a.   Robert Morse, in Jay Presson Allen's *Tru,* imitated the voice, appearance, and mannerisms of Truman Capote.
   b.   Richard Burbage put on the robes and manner of Richard III.
   c.   Jessica Lange dressed in the clothes of Blanche du Bois.
   * d.   In his portrayal of Clytemnestra, Polus carried his son's ashes onstage with him.
   360–361
   Brief: 62–63

103

6. Actors who feel the role from the inside, to the extent that they feel the feelings of the character and their entire physiology performs in addition to reproducing the actions of the character, are engaged in
   a. external mimesis.
   * b. embodiment of the character.
   c. self-reflection.
   d. meditation.
   361
   Brief: 63

7. When Plato says to Ion, "Are you not carried out of yourself, and does not your soul, in ecstasy, seem to be among the persons or the places of which you are speaking?" he is referring to a kind of possession which in acting is analogous to
   a. external mimesis.
   * b. embodiment.
   c. reflection.
   d. meditation.
   362
   Brief: 64

8. Which theorist maintained that only actors who were truly in love could effectively play lovers onstage unless they could develop a "happy insanity" that could persuade them that they were experiencing exactly what their characters seemed to experience?
   a. Aristotle
   b. Thespis
   * c. Saint Albine
   d. Denis Diderot
   363
   Brief: 65

9. Who maintained that the actor should be coldly unemotional? "At the moment when [the great actor] touches your heart he is listening to his own voice; his talent depends not, as you think, upon feeling, but upon rendering so exactly the outward signs of feeling that you fall into the trap. The broken voice, the half-uttered words, the stilted or prolonged notes [are all just] . . . magnificent apery."
   a. Aristotle
   * b. Denis Diderot
   c. Saint Albine
   d. Stanislavski
   363
   Brief: 65

10. The best acting synthesizes
   * a. the imitative and expressive sides of acting.
   b. the Dionysian and Apollonian roots of acting.
   c. simulation and embodiment.
   d. impersonation and virtuosity.
   363
   Brief: 65

11. What two features are required for a good actor?
   * a. a supple body and an expressive voice
   b. an expressive voice and a solid education in literature
   c. a solid education and self-possession on the stage
   d. an athletic body and a healthy mind
   364
   Brief: 66

 12. The personal resources of the actor that enable him or her to transcend the role through great skill and bring life to it are implied in the term
   a. credibility.
   b. imitation.
   * c. virtuosity.
   d. expressiveness.
   364
   Brief: 66

 13. Which of the following contributed to the decline of virtuosity in acting?
   a. the neoclassical emphasis on stylized acting forms
   * b. the rise of realism, which required that acting conform to the behaviors of ordinary people
   c. the modern renewed interest in rhetoric and declamation
   d. the aesthetics of performance art, which supplanted any interest in impersonation
   365
   Brief: 66

14. Which of the following does NOT contribute to the actor's magic, charisma, presence?
   * a. technical virtuosity
   b. inner confidence
   c. mastery of the craft
   d. inborn talent
   366
   Brief: 68

 15. The actor's instrument is the
   a. voice.
   b. body.
   * c. self.
   d. wardrobe.
   367
   Brief: 69

 16. Which of the following is NOT an element of voice?
   a. breathing
   b. phonation
   c. resonance
   * d. suppleness
   367
   Brief: 69

17. Which of the following is NOT an element of speech?
a. articulation
b. pronunciation
c. projection
* d. mastication
367
Brief: 69

 18. The major psychological component of the actor's instrument is
* a. imagination.
b. the unconscious.
c. memory.
d. discipline.
371
Brief: 73

 19. The actor's ability to use imagination to bring life to performance must be enhanced by the actor's application of the faculty of
a. credibility.
* b. discipline.
c. memory.
d. voice.
372
Brief: 74

20. Konstantin Stanislavski, founder of the Moscow Art Theatre (1898), said, "You must live the life of your character on stage." By this he was referring to
a. external mimesis.
* b. internal mimesis.
c. personification.
d. credibility.
373
Brief: 75

21. Which two writers best exemplify the range of difference between external and internal approaches to assuming a character?
* a. Diderot and Stanislavski
b. Thoreau and Aristotle
c. Thespis and Stanislavski
d. Diderot and Thoreau
373
Brief: 75

 22. American acting follows the school of
a. Aristotle.
b. Diderot.
* c. Stanislavski.
d. Cicero.
374
Brief: 76

23. How does Lee Strasberg's school of method acting differ from the Stanislavski school from which it derives?
    * a. Strasberg privileged the actor over the dramatic character.
    b. Strasberg privileged the dramatic character over the actor.
    c. Strasberg emphasized a history of style, whereas Stanislavski fostered a wholly individual approach.
    d. Strasberg emphasized voice, whereas Stanislavski emphasized physical body movements.
    375
    Brief: 77

24. Method actors have included
    a. Will Kemp and Richard Burbage.
    b. Lilly Langtree.
    * c. Marilyn Monroe and Marlon Brando.
    d. Nell Gwynne.
    375
    Brief: 77

25. The integrated methods of approach favored by today's teachers of acting emphasize
    * a. the situational intentions of the character that influence the tactics the character can employ.
    b. the unconscious, past motivation of the character that erupts into the present.
    c. the social forces that pressure the character into behaving in one way or another.
    d. the economic pressures placed on the character that determine his or her choices.
    375
    Brief: 77

26. "Situational intentions" refers to
    a. the influence of the past or the unconscious.
    * b. what the character desires to achieve, which pulls him forward toward a goal.
    c. the influence of the past, which propels the character from behind.
    d. the temporal and geographical context for the production.
    375
    Brief: 77

27. When the actor assesses the response he or she hopes to elicit from the audience, whether it be to empathize with the audience, alienate them, or instruct them, he or she is dealing with
    a. situational intentions.
    b. tactics.
    * c. mode of performance.
    d. impersonation.
    377
    Brief: 79

28. How successful was Brecht's theory of acting, which promulgated the idea that the actor alienate himself from the character and from the audience?
    a. Brecht's actors were consistently successful in preventing audience engagement with the character.
  * b. Brecht's actors were unsuccessful in preventing engagement with the character.
    c. Brecht's actors dropped out of character completely, and so his theory never had a chance at implementation.
    d. Brecht never attempted to implement his theory, so no knowledge is available about its efficacy.
    377
    Brief: 79

29. The three stages of the actor's routine are
    a. make-up, costume, and hair design.
    b. voice, body, and facial expressions.
  * c. auditioning, rehearsing, and performing.
    d. performing, producing, and criticizing.
    378
    Brief: 80

30. When the actor has the opportunity to demonstrate to the director how well he or she can fulfill the desired role by presenting a prepared reading or a cold reading from the script whose production is planned, the actor is in
  * a. audition.
    b. performance.
    c. rehearsal.
    d. abeyance.
    378
    Brief: 80

31. The ideal audition piece consists of
  * a. one- or two-minute monologues from plays or short narrative cuttings from novels, stories, or poems.
    b. a five-minute extended declamation, usually a soliloquy taken from the work of a major author.
    c. a two-minute speech combined with a song and dance to show the actor's speaking and moving range.
    d. a song and a dance only, set to lively music with a low bass.
    378
    Brief: 80

32. Which of the following does the director NOT look for in audition?
    a. actor's ease at handling the role
    b. naturalness of delivery
    c. physical, vocal, and emotional suitability for the part
  * d. ability to memorize lines
    380
    Brief: 82

33. Blocking refers to
   a. stage movements.
   b. dialogues.
   c. loudness of voice.
   d. quality of pronunciation.
   380
   Brief: 82

34. The customary rehearsal time for American professional productions is
   a. three to five weeks of forty-hour weeks.
   b. three to five weeks of twenty-hour weeks.
   c. two weeks, eighteen hours a day.
   d. five days of twenty-hour days.
   380
   Brief: 82

35. As the actor studies the role, he or she studies all of the following EXCEPT
   a. the subtext (the unspoken communication).
   b. the character's thoughts, fears, and fantasies.
   c. the world envisaged by the play and the playwright.
 * d. the playwright's family background.
   380
   Brief: 82

36. The French word for rehearsal is
   a. *dénouement.*
 * b. *répétition.*
   c. *sang froid.*
   d. *dessiner.*
   381
   Brief: 83

37. The practice of holding back until opening night is
   a. universally disavowed today.
   b. universally adopted today.
   c. adopted in regional theatre but not in Broadway productions.
   d. adopted in Broadway but not in regional theatre.
   381
   Brief: 83

38. The quality that describes the actor's ability to merge the character and the self to create the impression that both are real in time and place is
   a. mimesis.
   b. credibility.
   c. simulation.
 * d. presence.
   383
   Brief: 85

39. Performance technique, or the ability to read an audience,
    a. is learned.
    b. is intuited.
*   c. is usually instinctive but is enhanced by learning.
    d. is feigned.
    383
    Brief: 85

40. Unlike film actors, a problem common to stage actors is that
    a. stage actors lose weight during performances and have to change their eating habits.
*   b. stage actors find it difficult to maintain a high degree of spontaneity.
    c. stage actors tend to suffer from lapses in memory requiring them to re-memorize their parts.
    d. stage actors age during long performance runs and have to constantly change their make-up.
    383–384
    Brief: 85–86

41. Which of the following is NOT a way an actor may renew his or her relationship with the character?
    a. total immersion in the life of the character
    b. technical experiments by reworking delivery and finding new ways to say lines
    c. concentration on relationships within the play in order to find something new
*   d. concentration on relationships outside the play in order to enhance the range of feeling
    384
    Brief: 86

42. Stage fright is
    a. totally groundless and based on irrational fears.
*   b. a legitimate fear.
    c. a phobia transmitted genetically.
    d. a dietary disorder.
    384
    Brief: 86

43. "Acting addiction" refers to
    a. a person who cannot stop going to plays.
*   b. the actor obsessed with acting for its own sake.
    c. the person on the street who believes he or she is a famous actor from the past.
    d. a person who compulsively reads play reviews.
    385
    Brief: 87

44. The first actor was
    a. Aristotle.
    b. Diderot.
    c. Sophocles.
*   d. Thespis.
    360
    Brief: 62

45. According to Aristotle, tragedy is an imitation of
    a. a character.
    b. a situation.
*   c. an action.
    d. a theme.
    360
    Brief: 62

46. Why did the Greek actor Polus, when playing the role of Clytemnestra, bring the ashes of his dead son onstage with him?
    a. He wanted public acknowledgment of his son's death.
*   b. He wanted to summon up genuine feelings of grief.
    c. He wanted to elicit feelings of sympathy from the audience.
    d. He was trying to shock the audience.
    361
    Brief: 63

47. Etymologically, "emotion" refers to
    a. the actor's physical moving about on the stage.
*   b. the "out-motion" of humors.
    c. the actor's bringing out his personal history.
    d. the evocation or calling of the gods.
    362
    Brief: 64

48. In the classical Greek theatre, actors were given prizes for
    a. their physiques.
    b. their costumes.
*   c. their voices.
    d. their acrobatics.
    364
    Brief: 66

49. The training of the actor's instrument is
    a. physiological.
    b. literary and emotional.
*   c. psychological and physiological.
    d. psychological.
    367
    Brief: 69

50. Inhalation, practically understood as an element of voice, is sometimes seen to be mystically equivalent to
    a. imagination.
    b. virtuosity.
*   c. inspiration.
    d. credibility.
    368
    Brief: 70

51. Discuss the difference between external mimesis and embodiment. How much of the character is the actor? How much of character is the character as written by the playwright?

52. Discuss the importance of the actor's physical body—including physical prowess, strength, and virtuosity—to his or her career.

53. Discuss the role of imagination for acting. How does it come into play in the process of acting? Are there any limits on imagination?

54. Discuss the relationship between the actor's situational intentions, tactics, and mode of performance. How does this notion of a character's being drawn into a play by the attraction of a future goal or aim differ from a psychological orientation that maintains that humans are motivated by reacting to their past conflicts?

55. Imagine that you are preparing for an audition. Select your performance piece, then explain (1) how you would prepare it and (2) what aspects of your own ability this piece would demonstrate.

Chapter 12 / Brief: Chapter 4
The Playwright

1. One difference between the playwright in Shakespeare's time and the contemporary playwright is that
   * a. the playwright no longer functions as a director but is now considered an independent artist.
   b. the playwright no longer functions as an individual artist but is now considered part of a larger troupe.
   c. the playwright has always been an individual artist.
   d. the playwright has always been a member of a collaborative or collective economic and artistic body.
   389
   Brief: 91

2. The most important trait of the playwright is his or her
   a. fidelity to the rules of art.
   * b. intellectual independence.
   c. economic independence.
   d. advanced education.
   389
   Brief: 91

3. Every person is a playwright because
   * a. the unconscious stages an association of words and ideas when we sleep.
   b. child's play with dolls or cars shows the origin of the playwright's impulse.
   c. in everyday life, everyone plays a role.
   d. each person imaginatively creates a script he or she wants others to fulfill.
   389
   Brief: 91

4. Where have the most important American plays of the 1980s originally been presented?
   a. in off-Broadway productions under the direction of agents
   * b. in readings or workshops that solicit original works
   c. in regional theatres as part of collective independent theatre companies that generate their own scripts, much as Shakespeare generated scripts from his company
   d. in Broadway productions through the influence of heavily financed producers
   390
   Brief: 92

5. The purpose of a "developmental" theatrical company like the National Playwright's Conference is
*   a. to present staged readings of emerging writers.
    b. to present revival plays and invite new playwrights to comment on them.
    c. to hold a lottery to permit playwrights with all degrees of experience to have a chance at play presentation.
    d. to create situations in which a number of writers may collaborate on a single work.
    391
    Brief: 93

6. "Playwright" refers to
    a. a person who writes a play, as a novelist writes a novel.
    b. a person whose knowledge of dramaturgy is so skilled that he or she is always right.
*   c. a person who constructs or composes a play, as a wheelwright makes a wheel.
    d. a person whose sense of dialogue is so adept that it verges on a musical talent.
    391
    Brief: 93

7. The core of every play is
    a. character.
*   b. action.
    c. language.
    d. theme.
    392
    Brief: 94

8. The playwright works with two tools:
    a. the psychology of the characters and the viewpoint of the author.
    b. the impact of the social environment and the audience's sense of values.
    c. the actors and the set designer.
*   d. dialogue and physical action.
    392
    Brief: 94

9. A play in which events are connected to each other in strict chronological cause-effect continuity and in which dramatic experience attempts to convey a lifelike progression of experience through time is said to be
    a. discontinuous and linear.
    b. continuous and nonlinear.
    c. discontinuous and linear.
*   d. continuous and linear.
    392
    Brief: 94

10. Which of the following illustrates a linear plot?
    a. the *liaison de scènes* of Renaissance theatre
    b. the choral odes of Greek drama
    c. the prologue in a Shakespearean play
 * d. the didactic subtext of the lecture hall in Brecht's plays
    393
    Brief: 95

 11. The audience's demand for internal consistency in a play in which the characters, the situation, and the theatrical context are combined to generate the action creates
    a. economy.
    b. verisimilitude.
    c. virtuosity.
 * d. credibility.
    393
    Brief: 95

 12. That quality of a play that creates suspense by making us wonder what will happen next is called
    a. credibility.
 * b. intrigue.
    c. curiosity.
    d. awe.
    394
    Brief: 96

13. Which of the following is NOT an example of a play that reduces suspense?
    a. Greek plays that retell well-known myths
    b. the prologue to Shakespeare's *Romeo and Juliet*, which advises the audience about the outcome of the play
    c. Peter Shaffer's *Equus*, in which the most significant incident is described early in the play
 * d. the murder mystery *Murder on the Orient Express*
    395
    Brief: 97

 14. Which of the following is the most accurate statement of the audience's response to the drama?
    a. Surprise draws us into the world of the play; economy keeps us there.
    b. Credibility draws us into the world of the play; intrigue keeps us there.
    c. Curiosity draws us into the world of the play; realism keeps us there.
 * d. Intrigue draws us into the world of the play; credibility keeps us there.
    395
    Brief: 97

15. The quality of stage dialogue that makes it achieve maximum impact when spoken and that requires the playwright to be attentive to the audial shape of language, including the meaning of the dialogue and the rhythm of sound, is
    a. stageability.
    b. credibility.
*   c. speakability.
    d. actability.
    397
    Brief: 99

16. The quality of dialogue that describes its ability to function in the context of a particular physical situation in which setting, physical action, and spoken dialogue are inextricably entwined is called
*   a. stageability.
    b. credibility.
    c. speakability.
    d. definability.
    398
    Brief: 100

17. Which of the following is true of playwrighting activity in bygone days?
*   a. Playwrighting was considered so technically demanding that craft appeared to be all that was involved and playwrights spent long in-house apprenticeships as "company men," learning their skills through continual exposure in theatrical rehearsal and performance.
    b. Playwrighting was considered the work of amateurs and the favorite hobby of the landed gentry, who had vast amounts of leisure time.
    c. Playwrighting was thought to be divinely inspired, and playwrights were encouraged to seek inspiration in holy places like Jerusalem and Athens.
    d. Playwrighting was considered "not manly," and male playwrights were socially scorned.
    399
    Brief: 101

18. The quality of playwrighting that describes the way that every detail fortifies our insight into the play is called
*   a. richness.
    b. stageability.
    c. speakability.
    d. credibility.
    399
    Brief: 101

116

19. A play in which every character possesses an independence of intention, expression, and motivation that appears sensible in the light of our general knowledge of him or her is characterized by
    a. gravity.
 * b. depth of characterization.
    c. pertinence.
    d. stageability.
    400
    Brief: 102

20. All of the following are signs of good characterization EXCEPT
 * a. the character appears as an integer in the playwright's grand design.
    b. the characters convey the impression that they believe in themselves and in the fundamental rightness of their cause even though other characters or the audience may disagree with that estimation.
    c. even though haunted by self-doubts, the character sustains a belief in himself or herself.
    d. the character conveys the complexities of real human beings.
    400–401
    Brief: 102–103

21. Which quality of character began in realism and grew to become the dominant aspect of the theatrical experience by the mid-twentieth century, most notably in the plays of Tennessee Williams, William Inge, and Arthur Miller?
 * a. the role of the unconscious or psychoanalysis
    b. an awareness of the importance of social class and economics
    c. an awareness of the intrinsic competitiveness of the human situation
    d. the awe and humility felt when humanity senses itself in the presence of the divine
    401
    Brief: 103

22. When a play deals with an issue of serious and lasting significance in humanity's spiritual or intellectual life, it is said to possess
    a. credibility.
 * b. gravity.
    c. pertinence.
    d. stageability.
    401
    Brief: 103

23. A play that relates in some fashion to current personal concerns of the audience is said to possess
    a. credibility.
    b. gravity.
 * c. pertinence.
    d. speakability.
    401
    Brief: 103

24. The playwright's skill at condensing a story (which may span many days or even years of chronological time) into a theatrical time frame is called
   * a. compression.
   b. elaboration.
   c. intensity.
   d. gravity.
   402
   Brief: 104

25. The word that describes the playwright's skill at eliminating or consolidating characters, events, locales, and words in the interest of compression is called
   a. pertinence.
   * b. economy.
   c. intensity.
   d. gravity.
   402
   Brief: 104

26. What should the playwright do with events that are integral to the story but that cannot be shown within the devised setting?
   a. The playwright should delete any event that cannot be shown.
   b. The playwright should consult with the set designer in order to reconfigure the stage so that the event *can* be shown.
   * c. The playwright should report or narrate the event.
   d. The playwright should tape the event and play it back on a television monitor onstage.
   403
   Brief: 105

27. In what ways do dramatic economy and compression in the script NOT contribute to the overall staging of the play?
   a. They contribute to the intensity of the staged experience.
   b. They minimize the cost of production.
   c. They focus the plot, enhancing the audience's sense of intrigue.
   * d. They lengthen the playing time.
   403
   Brief: 105

28. What is the best place to start writing a play?
   a. Begin with the facts.
   b. Begin with the characters.
   c. Begin with the plot.
   * d. Everyone begins differently.
   405
   Brief: 107

29. A dramatic exercise that enhances the playwright's ability to write consists of
    *   a.   moving from remembered dialogue to imagined dialogue.
        b.   moving from imagined dialogue to remembered dialogue.
        c.   a concept that is worked out from beginning to end.
        d.   outlining the plot in proper form.
        405–406
        Brief: 107–108

30. Scenes of forced conflict are important because
    *   a.   climactic scenes define structure, character, and situation.
        b.   these scenes display the playwright's virtuosity.
        c.   such scenes bracket theatrical pauses or breaks that can accommodate commercials should the
             script go to film.
        d.   no conflict ever comes naturally.
        407–408
        Brief: 109–110

31. Which quality is possessed by the play?
    *   a.   credibility
        b.   gravity
        c.   independence
        d.   economy
        393
        Brief: 95

32. Which of the following attributes applies only to the playscript itself?
    *   a.   linearity
        b.   virtuosity
        c.   independence
        d.   credibility
        393
        Brief: 95

33. Which attribute applies to the playwright?
    *   a.   independent thought and vision
        b.   economy
        c.   stageability
        d.   speakability
        395
        Brief: 97

34. What aspect of the play CANNOT be represented through dialogue?
    *   a.   a character's improvisation or comic behavior
        b.   a character's irony
        c.   a character's attitude
        d.   a character's relationship to others
        391
        Brief: 93

35. Which of the following is an example of a play that is discontinuous and nonlinear?
    * a. Joan Littlewood's *Oh, What a Lovely War!*
      b. Sophocles' *Oedipus Tyrannos*
      c. Congreve's *The Way of the World*
      d. Racine's *Phadre*
      393
      Brief: 95

36. James Barrie's play *Peter Pan* deals with characters that are wholly appropriate to their imaginary situation and internally consistent in their actions within the context of the play. This play may be said to make a picture of a real world, and thus this play possesses
      a. levity.
      b. gravity.
      c. pertinence.
    * d. credibility.
      393
      Brief: 95

37. The importance of psychiatric action has stood at the center of all the plays EXCEPT which of the following?
      a. Peter Shaffer's *Equus*
      b. Arthur Miller's *After the Fall*
      c. Tennessee Williams's *Suddenly Last Summer*
    * d. Arthur Miller's *Death of a Salesman*
      401
      Brief: 103

38. When did the image of the playwright move from that of theatrical coworker to that of the isolated observer and social critic?
      a. from the Restoration onward
      b. from the Baroque onward
    * c. since the age of romanticism
      d. since the modern era
      389
      Brief: 91

39. One book that is particularly informative as a guide to dramatic contests, commercial reading and critique services, and literary/dramatic agents is
      a. *The Research Guide to the Theatre.*
    * b. *Dramatists Sourcebook.*
      c. *Grant's Handbook.*
      d. *Merck Manual.*
      391
      Brief: 93

120

40. Which element of literature is NOT important in drama?
    a. poetic allusion
    b. alliteration and rhyme
    c. narrative structure
    * d. legibility
    392
    Brief: 94

41. A play with which type of plot was the neoclassical ideal?
    * a. a linear continuous plot
    b. a nonlinear continuous plot
    c. a nonlinear discontinuous plot
    d. a linear noncontinuous plot
    392
    Brief: 94

42. A linear plot proceeds by
    * a. point-to-point storytelling.
    b. one episode jumping to another.
    c. one character's passing a symbol or token to another.
    d. one image fading into another image.
    393
    Brief: 95

43. The quality of a play that refers to a continual stream of information is called
    a. speakability.
    * b. flow.
    c. linearity.
    d. progression.
    399
    Brief: 101

44. Fill in the blank: Compression is to playwright as _____ is to script.
    * a. economy
    b. verisimilitude
    c. credibility
    d. independence
    402
    Brief: 104

45. Ultimately, a play should
    a. celebrate life.
    b. analyze life.
    c. criticize life.
    d. ironize life.
    403
    Brief: 105

46. "Theatre of fact" usually begins with
    * a. a real-life character.
    b. a document such as the transcript of a trial.
    c. a myth, such as the archetypal story of the scapegoat.
    d. the playwright's dream vision.
    405
    Brief: 107

47. Which of the following is true of the relationship between literary brilliance and playwrighting?
    a. Literary eloquence is the most important criterion of a play.
    * b. A pretext for great acting, even if the language is minimalist, is more important than literary excellence.
    c. Alliteration and poetic verse are the most important aspect of playwrighting because the poetic meters govern the actor's voice.
    d. Irony, a crucial element to any drama, can only be conveyed through language, which, while not beautiful, must be compelling, even to the extent of sacrificing action.
    392
    Brief: 94

48. When intrigue demanding surprise and credibility demanding consistency combine together they create a fundamental state of the drama called
    a. serendipitous discovery.
    b. wonderful surprise.
    * c. believable wonder.
    d. understandable dilemma.
    395
    Brief: 97

49. Which play, published in 1953, radically "rewrote the book" on playwrighting by offering actors and directors new lessons about what is speakable and stageable?
    a. John Millington Synge's *Riders to the Sea*
    * b. Samuel Beckett's *Waiting for Godot*
    c. Peter Shaffer's *Equus*
    d. Tennessee Williams's *Cat on a Hot Tin Roof*
    399
    Brief: 101

50. When a playwright has managed to make every scene, every incident, every character, and every word deliver an impact, he or she has satisfied the dramatic demand for
    a. believability.
    * b. intensity.
    c. credibility.
    d. intrigue.
    402
    Brief: 104

ESSAY QUESTIONS

51. Discuss the attributes of a good playscript. Consider the elements of story or narrative, the element of played or performed text, and the practical requirements of a stage.

52. Visit your local theatre and playing company, then take a play like Shakespeare's *Romeo and Juliet* (or another play of your choice), and discuss it in terms of its speakability and stageability with respect to a particular theatre you know.

53. Visit a production of a local repertory theatre, and interview the producer there. How does the producer make decisions about the plays that theatre will put on? For instance, are there physical limitations to the actual stage or economic limitations that will make the producer prefer one kind of play to another?

54. Let's imagine that you are going to write a play and you have just come up with a general concept: this play is about a love triangle. During the course of the play, all the members of the triangle will change their affections, but, by the end, each person in the triangle will revert to the position held at the beginning of the play. Make an outline showing how you would develop this concept. You may go so far as to draw character sketches and write dialogue.

55. Take the following lines from Shakespeare's *King Lear,* and explain how they relate to the criteria for speakability, stageability, compression, and intrigue: "Howl howl."

56. Go through the following exercise already discussed in the chapter: Write two pages of remembered dialogue; building on that, add two pages of imagined dialogue, which in turn leads to a scene of forced conflict.

Chapter 13 / Brief: Chapter 5
Designers and Technicians

1. Realistic costuming took over when which of the following became a major guiding principle in drama?
   a. the expression of the individual consciousness
   b. social expression
   * c. historical accuracy
   d. psychological accuracy
   436
   Brief: 138

2. In *commedia dell'arte,* costuming was used to
   * a. identify a character type.
   b. reflect the theme of the play.
   c. simply dress the character.
   d. reflect the psychological processes of the individual.
   436
   Brief: 138

3. This member of the company has the job of overseeing all elements of production, including coordinating the director's work with that of the actors, scheduling calls, recording the blocking, and organizing the basic "calling" of the show.
   * a. production manager
   b. director
   c. technical director
   d. assistant director
   450
   Brief: 152

4. One Greek theatre that survives from the fourth century B.C. and that continues to be used as a playing site for revivals is
   a. the Theatre of Dionysus at the foot of the Acropolis in Athens.
   b. the Greco-Roman amphitheatre in Palermo.
   * c. the theatre at Epidaurus.
   d. the Theatre of the Four Winds in Thessaly.
   412
   Brief: 114

5. The architect of Shakespeare's Globe Theatre and Henslowe's Fortune Theatre was
   a. Andrea Palladio.
   * b. Peter Street.
   c. Christopher Wren.
   d. Frank Gehry.
   412
   Brief: 114

6. The Teatro Olimpico, built in Vicenza, Italy (1584), is the best known example of the architect
    a. Peter Street.
*   b. Andrea Palladio.
    c. Christopher Wren.
    d. Calamity Jones.
    412–413
    Brief: 114–115

7. Another term for the picture-frame stage is the
    a. *trompe l'oeil.*
    b. *mise en abyme.*
    c. Palladian set.
*   d. proscenium stage.
    413
    Brief: 115

8. The picture-frame stage reached its highest realization in the
*   a. Renaissance.
    b. Victorian era.
    c. Restoration.
    d. Postmodern era.
    414
    Brief: 116

9. Which of the following is an actor-centered (rather than a scenery-centered) type of stage?
    a. medieval *mansions*
    b. proscenium arch stage
*   c. thrust stage
    d. arena format
    414
    Brief: 116

10. Which type of stage dispenses with all scenery except floor treatments, furniture, and out-of-the-way standing or hanging pieces to focus attention on the actors?
*   a. arena format
    b. black box
    c. thrust stage
    d. proscenium
    414–415
    Brief: 116–117

11. This kind of stage consists of a bare room fitted with omni-flexible overhead lighting in which stage and seating can be configured in various arrangements and that accommodates a range of dramas including happenings and participatory rituals.
   a. arena stage
   b. thrust stage
   c. proscenium stage
* d. black box
   415
   Brief: 117

12. In the Greek drama, rotating prisms, rolling platforms, and painted panels
* a. probably had no representational significance.
   b. represented the actual location of the drama.
   c. represented the world of the audience.
   d. represented the world of the court.
   416
   Brief: 118

 13. The development of _____ fostered the great period of scenery design.
   a. the thrust stage
   b. the medieval platform stage
* c. the illuminated indoor theatre
   d. the Roman open air theatre
   416
   Brief: 118

 14. Make-up serves all the functions EXCEPT which of the following?
   a. Illustrative make-up is the means by which the actor converts his appearance to resemble that of the character.
   b. Make-up may be used to evoke or highlight psychological traits.
   c. Make-up may simplify or embolden the actor's features in order to make them distinct and expressive to every member of the audience.
* d. Make-up may be used to help improve the actor's diction.
   433–435
   Brief: 145–147

15. Which of the following people is NOT a scenery designer?
   a. Aristotile da Sangallo
   b. Giacomo Torelli
   c. Inigo Jones
* d. Christopher Wren
   417
   Brief: 119

16. What kind of set would be filled with real furniture and real properties taken from ordinary real-world environments?
    * a. illusionist set
    b. symbolist set
    c. naturalist set
    d. expressionist set
    417–418
    Brief: 119–120

17. The type of set that fostered a uniquely architectural theory of theatre was
    * a. theatre with one wall removed.
    b. floor-to-ceiling drama.
    c. homeism.
    d. cyclorama.
    419
    Brief: 121

18. The movement toward scenic abstraction began with the theoretical (and occasionally practical) works of
    a. Inigo Jones.
    b. Francisco Marinetti.
    * c. Adolphe Appia.
    d. Vsevolod Meyerhold.
    419
    Brief: 121

19. "Costume" comes from the same root as
    * a. "custom," meaning what the characters of a world habitually wear.
    b. "cosmos," as in "cosmetic," meaning the decoration added on to something.
    c. "costly," meaning any expensive type of adornment.
    d. "couture," meaning contemporary or in vogue.
    427
    Brief: 139

20. Which of the following is NOT a postmodern design element?
    a. random assemblages of different and unrelated styles
    b. found objects strewn on the set
    c. painted scenery made to look especially scenic
    * d. furniture taken directly from people's homes
    421
    Brief: 123

21. Speaking of dramatic space as "psycho-plastic," Europe's most celebrated "scenographer" has said, "The goal of a designer can no longer be a description of a copy of actuality, but the creation of its multidimensional model." Who is this person?

* a. Joseph Svoboda
   b. Arthur Kopit
   c. Jo Mielziner
   d. Elia Kazan
   423
   Brief: 125

22. Who performed "mute spectacles" in which whole performances were arranged with nothing but scene designs, lighting, and posed actors?

* a. Jean-Nicholas Servandoni
   b. Elia Kazan
   c. Arthur Kopit
   d. Jo Mielziner
   423
   Brief: 125

23. A piece of canvas stretched over a wooden frame and then painted to imitate vertical walls and to define spaces is called
   a. a proscenium.
   b. a cyclorama.
   c. a bustier.
* d. a flat.
   424
   Brief: 126

24. Which of the following is NOT a use for stage drapery?
   a. The opera drape, when lowered and raised, is used to signal the beginning and end of a production.
   b. A drapery border is used to mask the stage lighting above the set.
   c. A set of blacks is used to create the setting for readings, chamber productions, and reader's theatre productions.
* d. The stage drapery is frequently used as a piano cover when a performance is going on.
   424–425
   Brief: 126–127

25. A hanging fabric stretched taut between upper and lower pipes and curved to surround the rear and sides of the stage and colored with various colors, in part to represent a series of skyscapes, is called
   a. sky curtains.
   b. curtain wings.
* c. cyclorama.
   d. proscenium.
   425
   Brief: 127

26. Which person is responsible for the building and operation of stage machinery and scenery, has charge of lighting crews and industrial scheduling, has charge of moving scenery in and out of the theatre, and establishes policies and directives for scene shifting?
* a. technical director
b. dramaturge
c. production manager
d. director
450
Brief: 152

 27. A loosely woven fabric that looks opaque when lit from one side and transparent when lit from the other side is called
a. a cyclorama.
b. the missing fourth wall.
c. a convention.
* d. a scrim.
427
Brief: 129

28. Turntables, elevators, hoists, cranes, rolling carts, and wagons that are used as scenic elements to accompany and support the dramatic action are called
a. scrims.
b. portable sets.
* c. machinery.
d. cycloramas.
427
Brief: 129

 29. Make-up, like costuming, is
* a. both ceremonial and illustrative.
b. ceremonial alone.
c. illustrative alone.
d. nonsignifying.
443
Brief: 145

30. "Theatre" means
a. acting place.
b. scenic place.
c. playing space.
* d. seeing space.
428
Brief: 130

31. Which of the following is the most recent theatrical innovation in staging?
    a. lighting
    b. costuming
    * c. painted scenery
    d. make-up
    417, 428
    Brief: 119, 130

32. One of the first developers of flat painted scenery was
    * a. Sebastiano Serlio.
    b. Adolphe Appia.
    c. Christopher Wren.
    d. Inigo Jones.
    417, 429
    Brief: 119, 131

33. Which invention brought lighting to the stage in its modern form and made lighting a more controlled part of the drama?
    a. the three-tiered candelabra
    b. the kerosene lamp
    * c. the gaslight
    d. the use of tallow for candles
    429
    Brief: 131

34. When was electricity introduced into American theatres for lighting?
    * a. 1879
    b. 1901
    c. 1860
    d. 1753
    429
    Brief: 131

35. The primary considerations of lighting design are
    * a. visibility and focus.
    b. focus and clarity.
    c. clarity and obfuscation.
    d. clarity and dimension.
    431
    Brief: 133

36. The "theatricalist" use of lighting in Brecht's didactic theatre called for
    * a. the lighting instruments to be exposed and placed in full view of the audience.
    b. the lighting to be hidden in order to reinforce the moral of his plays.
    c. all other stage lights to be subsumed to the spotlight.
    d. "spotlight" to be written on a placard and passed back and forth among the speaking characters.
    431
    Brief: 133

37. A plan or series of plans showing the placement of each lighting instrument and its type, wattage, size, wiring and connection to a dimmer, and color is called
   a. a scrim.
   b. a cyclorama.
 * c. a light plot.
   d. a light plan.
   433
   Brief: 135

 38. A list of occasions referred to by number and keyed to the script of the play in which lights change either in intensity or in their use is called
   a. a light plot.
 * b. a cue sheet.
   c. a cue plan.
   d. a flowsheet.
   434
   Brief: 136

 39. Thin, transparent sheets of plastic placed over a light to change its color are called
   a. light plots.
 * b. gelatins.
   c. filters.
   d. rainbow plastic.
   435
   Brief: 137

40. The first theatrical costumes were
   a. the actual clothes of the actors.
 * b. ceremonial vestments.
   c. the clothes of patrons, who donated them to the theatre.
   d. military uniforms.
   435
   Brief: 137

41. The thick-soled footwear of the Greek actors, used in the fourth century and intended to increase their height, were called
   a. *himation.*
 * b. *kothurnoi.*
   c. *catharsis.*
   d. *alb.*
   435–436
   Brief: 137–138

 42. The ancient and original use of costume was to
   a. make the actor resemble a character.
 * b. separate the actor from the audience.
   c. make the actor blend into the setting.
   d. conceal the effects of pox or plague on the actor's face.
   435
   Brief: 137

ESSAY QUESTIONS

43. Discuss the range and features of stage lighting.

44. Take a scene or an action from a play, and discuss how you would stage it for the thrust stage and for the proscenium stage. Then, in a separate section, discuss the differences in the two kinds of staging.

45. Aeschylus's play *Agamemnon* was staged so that the watchman's spotting of the signal fire (which heralded Agamemnon's return to Argo) coincided with the actual sunrise over the Athenian *skene* (playhouse). Discuss two ways to use artificial lighting and staging to accommodate this opening. One way should evoke a realistic effect, and one should create an expressionist or symbolic effect.

46. Discuss the role of costuming to show a character's conformity or nonconformity of style with respect to other characters in a play. Then take a scene from a play of your choice, and explain how you would costume the characters to show conformity and nonconformity; then explain what difference costuming shows in the character.

47. Compare and contrast the advantages and limitations of the thrust stage with those of the black box set.

Chapter 14 / Brief: Chapter 6
The Director

 1. Which of the following tasks belongs to the director?
    a.   arranging the financial backing to perform the play
    b.   arranging for the scenery and props
    c.   hiring the producer
*   d.   conceptualizing the play and giving it vision and purpose
    452
    Brief: 154

 2. Which of the following is true of the director's role?
    a.   Directing has always been a defined role within the theatre company.
    b.   Directing is an innovation in drama that accompanied the proscenium stage.
*   c.   There has always been a director but not always an individual specifically charged with that role.
    d.   Directing was done by a triumvirate in Greek times.
    452
    Brief: 154

3. In the earliest days of theatre, theatre was considered a form of
    a.   entertainment.
    b.   ritual.
*   c.   teaching.
    d.   government.
    452
    Brief: 154

4. The Greek word for director was
*   a.   *didaskalos,* meaning "teacher."
    b.   *himation,* meaning "holy one."
    c.   *spargasmos,* meaning "dividing into parts."
    d.   *tyrannos,* meaning "leader."
    452
    Brief: 154

 5. When did the teacher-director reach an historical pinnacle of influence?
    a.   early Roman times
    b.   mid-Medieval times
*   c.   Enlightenment and Victorian periods
    d.   Renaissance and early Restoration periods
    453
    Brief: 155

6. How did the eighteenth- and nineteenth-centuries' emphasis on rationalism influence the director's role?
   * a. The demand for historical accuracy required the director to conduct comprehensive research, organization, and coordination.
   b. The high cost of true-to-life sets required the director to solicit patronage.
   c. Directors studied rhetoric and logic, which extended their education in theatre.
   d. Directors felt the need to study original dramatic theorists, and so many were compelled to study and learn French.
   453
   Brief: 155

7. André Antoine and Konstantin Stanislavski are primarily known as
   a. symbolists.
   b. realists.
   * c. naturalists.
   d. expressionists.
   454
   Brief: 156

8. Who is generally regarded as the first modern director?
   a. Alexander Pope
   * b. George II, Duke of Saxe-Meiningen
   c. Denis Diderot
   d. Franco Tonelli
   453
   Brief: 155

9. Which of the following is NOT known as an antirealist stylizing director/theorist?
   * a. André Antoine
   b. Paul Fort
   c. Vsevolod Meyerhold
   d. Gordon Craig
   454–455
   Brief: 156–157

10. What did André Antoine, George II, and Konstantin Stanislavski have in common?
    a. Working closely with architects, they designed their own theatres.
    * b. They theorized and worked pragmatically at organizing a theatre company.
    c. They founded actors' unions.
    d. They organized a retirement fund for professional members of the theatre.
    454
    Brief: 156

11. Which of the following directors opened up the theatre to possibilities of psychological interpretation?
   a. Antonin Artaud
   b. Clive Barnes
 * c. Harley Granville-Barker
   d. Paul Fort
   454
   Brief: 156

12. Which of the following founded the Théâtre d'Art in Paris in 1890 as a direct assault upon the realist principles espoused by André Antoine?
   a. David Belasco
   b. Otto Brahm
 * c. Paul Fort
   d. Christopher Lee
   454
   Brief: 156

13. Which of the following directors evolved his theatre of "biomechanical constructivism" in Moscow as a response against Stanislavski's realism?
   a. André Antoine
   b. Antonin Artaud
 * c. Vsevolod Meyerhold
   d. Joseph Svoboda
   454
   Brief: 156

14. Which of the following is true of the stylizing directors?
   a. They are led by the goals of realism taken to an extreme.
 * b. They are unrestrained by rigid formulas with respect to verisimilitude or realistic behavior.
   c. They are very well educated with a background in classical rhetoric and declamation.
   d. They adopt the ritual and forms of church influence.
   454
   Brief: 156

15. Who is the author of a seminal essay, "The Art of the Theatre" (1905), which compares the director of a play to a captain of a ship in the following lines: "Until discipline is understood in a theatre to be willing and reliant obedience to the manager [director] or captain, no supreme achievement can be accomplished"?
   a. Harley Granville-Barker
   b. Otto Brahm
   c. Joseph Svoboda
 * d. Gordon Craig
   455
   Brief: 157

16. Which person is responsible for the financial support of the production?
    a. producer
    b. director
    c. technical stage manager
    d. stage manager
    456
    Brief: 158

17. Which of the following is true of the regional theatre?
    a. The theatre's director is often an unpaid actor as well.
    * b. The theatre's artistic director normally serves as the producer of each production and the director of one or more plays.
    c. The theatre's producer has no other function than to raise funds for the seasons' performances.
    d. There is no producer in regional theatre.
    456
    Brief: 158

18. Who selects the plays, engages the artistic staff, and possibly casts the actors?
    a. director
    b. assistant director
    * c. producer
    d. artistic director
    457
    Brief: 159

19. Who is charged with the artistic vision and leadership?
    a. producer
    * b. director
    c. assistant director
    d. dramaturge
    457
    Brief: 159

20. Over which directorial decision does the producer have the most interest in retaining the right of review?
    a. casting
    b. stage design
    * c. play selection
    d. thematic direction
    458
    Brief: 160

21. The director directs all of the following EXCEPT
    a. the actors.
    b. the audience.
    c. the designers.
    * d. the producer.
    458
    Brief: 160

22. What is meant by the "concept" of a play?
    a. the central idea in the writer's mind
    b. the point of view of the popular audience
  * c. the director's central idea, which focuses his interpretation
    d. the critic's general reception of the play itself
    459
    Brief: 161

23. What is a traditional staging of Shakespeare?
    a. Peter Brook's twentieth-century version
    b. seventeenth-century revisionist staging
    c. nineteenth-century realistic staging
  * d. all stagings are speculative and creative
    459
    Brief: 161

24. Which of the following is NOT included in the conceptualization of a play?
    a. a social or philosophical statement about meaning
    b. a specific interpretation
    c. a basic tone or texture
  * d. the family history of the playwright
    460
    Brief: 162

25. Where does the director start in order to begin selecting designers and actors?
    a. with the musical score or sound requirements
    b. with a principal actor around whom the production may be organized
  * c. with the concept
    d. with the physical dimensions of the stage
    460
    Brief: 162

26. What does a director NOT seek in a designer-director collaboration?
    a. personal compatibility
    b. a synchrony of artistic and intellectual vision
    c. mutual respect
  * d. financial independence
    461
    Brief: 163

27. The director's and designer's goals are identical: they both concern themselves with all of the following EXCEPT
    a. actable space.
    b. wearable costumes.
    c. the evocative appearance of the whole.
  * d. the play selection.
    462
    Brief: 164

28. From the audience point of view, the one wholly unique ingredient of the production is
    a.   the scenery.
    b.   the script.
    c.   the lighting.
    *   d.   the actors.
    464
    Brief: 166

29. The director makes a decision about the actor in
    a.   a two- to four-minute cold audition.
    b.   a ten-minute prepared reading followed by a personal interview.
    c.   a review of the actor's portfolio.
    d.   a résumé and a short video.
    465
    Brief: 167

30. In the professional theatre, according to union requirements,
    *   a.   actors receive pay for fifth and ensuing calls.
    b.   actors are paid for every call after the first.
    c.   actors are not paid until they are definitively cast for the production.
    d.   actors are paid for every call.
    465
    Brief: 167

31. The timing and placement of a character's entrances, exits, crosses, embraces, and other major movements is called
    *   a.   blocking.
    b.   staging.
    c.   technical managing.
    d.   directing.
    467
    Brief: 169

32. Which of the following requires specialized blocking, perhaps even direction by a specialist?
    a.   an entrance through the wings
    b.   an exit through the wings
    *   c.   a duel
    d.   a soliloquy
    467–468
    Brief: 169–170

33. Small-scale movement on the stage, which a character performs within the larger pattern of entrances and exits, is called
    a.   blocking.
    *   b.   business.
    c.   producing.
    d.   managing.
    468
    Brief: 170

34. The director spends most of his time doing which of the following?
   a. selecting the play
   b. selecting the cast
* c. coaching the actors
   d. working with designers
   468
   Brief: 170

35. The theatrical word for teamwork is
   a. collaboration.
   b. dialogism.
   c. complicity.
* d. ensemble.
   469
   Brief: 171

36. The rhythm of a production, sometimes confused with the speed of the actor's delivery, is called
   a. style.
   b. mode.
* c. pace.
   d. verisimilitude.
   470
   Brief: 172

37. Which aspect of rehearsal—during which scenery, lighting, and sound are added—occurs near the end of the rehearsal process as the play comes closer to production time?
   a. audition
* b. technical rehearsal
   c. dress rehearsal
   d. blocking
   472
   Brief: 174

38. At what point in the audition/performance cycle does the director give up the production?
   a. auditioning
   b. rehearsal
   c. dress rehearsal
* d. final production
   472
   Brief: 174

39. The contemporary age has been called the "Age of the _____ ."
   a. Actor
   b. Playwright
* c. Director
   d. Stage Designer
   455
   Brief: 157

40. The directing process encompasses two phases:
    a. selection and implementation.
    b. hiring and firing.
    c. reading and acting.
    d. collecting money and allocating funds.
    458
    Brief: 160

41. The staging of a play includes
    a. hidden blocking effects.
    b. bold blocking effects.
*   c. hidden and bold blocking effects.
    d. no blocking effects.
    467
    Brief: 169

42. What determines the pace of a play?
    a. the number of lines or pages in the script
    b. the speed of the actor's delivery
*   c. the quality and quantity of information conveyed to the audience
    d. whether or not the play is being filmed
    470
    Brief: 172

43. Which of the following INCORRECTLY pairs a director with his or her previous profession?
    a. Elia Kazan: actor
    b. Gower Champion: choreographer
*   c. William Kemp: dancer
    d. Franco Zeffirelli: scene designer
    474
    Brief: 176

44. Which of the following is NOT a criterion for play selection?
    a. the director's interest
    b. the interest of the intended audience
    c. the capability of the director and producer to conceptualize and produce the play
*   d. the producer's ability to raise funds
    458
    Brief: 160

45. Who selects the designer?
    a. the producer
*   b. the director
    c. the assistant director
    d. the designer is already a member of the staff
    461
    Brief: 163

46. Which of the following is true of the relationships between actors and directors?
    a. In Restoration theatres, 90 percent of actors directed their own plays.
    b. According to Gordon Craig, a director should never set foot on the stage as an actor.
*   c. Some directors have started their careers as actors.
    d. The Stanislavski Method strictly prohibits actors from directing their own productions.
    474
    Brief: 176

47. How does the director's role differ in Broadway productions and university productions?
*   a. There is no difference.
    b. In university productions, major directorial decisions are made by academic committees.
    c. In university productions, the directors obtain a larger percentage of proceeds.
    d. Reviews of Broadway productions have traditionally paid little attention to the director.
    456
    Brief: 158

48. Which of the following is true about the way directorial concepts take shape?
    a. Existentialist anxiety plays no role.
    b. These concepts are usually clearly defined by the playwright.
    c. These concepts are usually determined by prevailing fashion.
*   d. These concepts are formed at the unconscious and conscious levels of the director's mind.
    459
    Brief: 161

49. What did *didaskalos* mean in medieval times?
    a. preacher
*   b. master
    c. conqueror
    d. speaker
    452–453
    Brief: 154–155

50. When did the concern for more lifelike productions spark a revision of theatrical conventions and the role of the director?
    a. the Enlightenment
    b. the beginning of the Elizabethan era
*   c. late nineteenth century
    d. the mid-1980s
    453
    Brief: 155

ESSAY QUESTIONS

51. Go through a play and pick out two scenes or phases of action that have different pacing needs. Then explain how you think the tempo should move and how that pacing relates to the immediate dramatic business that occurs at the moment.

52. Trace the role of the director as she or he works with a scene from the beginning of the play to the final production.

53. Imagine that you are a director planning a production. You have to decide on a play to produce. Pick a play you would like to direct, and explain (1) why you chose that play and (2) what concept you would choose to stage it. How would that concept make itself felt through stage design, costuming, and casting?

54. What are the three eras of directing? In an essay, explain each era and discuss the major contributions of specific directors in each period.

55. Describe the Stanislavski Method. Then speculate on its limitations or advantages for actors and for directors.

Chapter 15 / Brief: Chapter 9
The Critic

1. The formalization of postplay thinking and conversation is called
* a. dramatic criticism.
   b. literary criticism.
   c. semiotic criticism.
   d. poststructural criticism.
   476
   Brief: 292

2. Dramatic criticism usually appears in all of the following forms EXCEPT
   a. production reviews in newspapers or periodicals.
   b. essays about plays or play productions written as academic assignments.
* c. annotated versions of a playscript used in production.
   d. scholarly articles or books on dramatic literature.
   476
   Brief: 292

3. Why is the theatre in a strong position to force and focus public confrontation with social issues?
   a. The theatre artist, whose point of view generally turns to the left or to the right of mainstream views, offers an unusual perspective on the human condition.
   b. The theatre has traditionally served as an arena for the discussion of virtually any imaginable social issue.
* c. The best productions do not act as propaganda but present the issues in all their complexity as food for thought.
   d. The theatre has historically been connected with government institutions.
   477
   Brief: 293

4. Plays that deal with theatrical matter not simply as a vehicle but as a theme are called
* a. metadrama or metatheatre.
   b. hyperdrama or hypertheatre.
   c. hypodrama or hypotheatre.
   d. sur-drama or sur-theatre.
   480
   Brief: 296

5. Which of the following is NOT an example of a play that makes the theatre a topic in the play itself?
   a. Stoppard's *Rosencrantz and Guildenstern Are Dead*
   b. Pirandello's *Six Characters in Search of an Author*
   c. Shakespeare's *Hamlet*
* d. Sophocles' *Oedipus the King*
   480
   Brief: 296

6. What word best fits the definition of "that which holds the attention"?
   a. suspense
* b. entertainment
   c. tension
   d. anxiety
   482
   Brief: 298

7. A member of the audience may see a play from five different perspectives. What are they?
* a. social, personal, artistic, theatrical, entertainment value
   b. tragic, comic, satiric, ironic, tragic-comic
   c. pastoral, ironic, idyllic, epic, lyric
   d. thematic, characterological, dictional, spectacular, thaumaturgical
   483
   Brief: 299

8. What form does professional dramatic criticism take?
* a. Production reviews, scholarly books, and articles written, for the most part, by persons who specialize in this activity
   b. Group sessions between actors, directors, and producers
   c. Academic seminars
   d. Panel discussions among members of the audience following a performance
   483
   Brief: 299

9. The journalist's review generally is
   a. extended to a detailed and exhaustive study based on consultation with critical articles.
* b. limited to a brief, immediate reaction written within a few days of seeing the performance.
   c. an extended discussion based not only on his impressions of the play but also on interviews with the actors and playwright.
   d. based on a consensus of audience reactions.
   485
   Brief: 301

10. Which of the following is the newspaper critic's principal job qualification?
   a. dramatic expertise
* b. writing skill
   c. playwrighting or directing experience
   d. willingness to attend performances
   485
   Brief: 301

11. Scholarly critics generally write
  * a. detailed, comprehensive, and rigorously researched articles without deadlines or space limitations.
    b. without concern for the published opinions of other critics and scholars.
    c. erudite apologia for their own biases.
    d. historical surveys that strictly avoid judgments of taste.
    485
    Brief: 301

12. A "scholar" is
    a. one who psychoanalyzes.
    b. one who observes.
  * c. one who studies.
    d. one who considers.
    485
    Brief: 301

13. Which of the following was NOT known as a drama critic?
    a. Aristotle
    b. Goethe
  * c. Husserl
    d. Nietzsche
    485
    Brief: 301

14. The professional scholar
    a. is content to repeat the opinions or discoveries of others.
    b. writes from his or her own intuition.
  * c. seeks fresh insights from a body of literature while working within accepted methodologies.
    d. depends entirely upon received opinions and public consensus.
    485
    Brief: 301

15. Which methodology is NOT one that grew up in the 1970s?
    a. structuralist
    b. semiotic
    c. deconstructive
  * d. psychoanalytic
    485
    Brief: 301

16. Which critic attends the performance with an open mind and sharply tuned senses?
    a. informed critic
  * b. observant critic
    c. sensitive critic
    d. demanding critic
    490
    Brief: 306

17. Which critic is sensitive to life and artistic experience and has a compassionate approach toward life, humankind, and artistic expression that elicits a personalized response to dramatic works?
    a. observant critic
    b. informed critic
  * c. sensitive critic
    d. demanding critic
    490
    Brief: 306

18. Which critic needs sufficient background to provide a context for opinion and evaluation? His or her judgments are made against a background of knowledge and experience.
    a. observant critic
  * b. informed critic
    c. sensitive critic
    d. demanding critic
    490
    Brief: 306

19. Which critic holds the theatre to its highest possible standards and thus cuts against the inherent danger in drama to turn toward pure entertainment or sensationalism?
    a. observant critic
    b. informed critic
    c. articulate critic
  * d. demanding critic
    490
    Brief: 306

20. Which critic expresses thoughts with precision, clarity, and grace through the careful building up of ideas through a presentation of evidence, logical argument, the use of helpful analogy and example, and a clear style of expression?
    a. observant critic
  * b. articulate critic
    c. sensitive critic
    d. demanding critic
    490
    Brief: 306

ESSAY QUESTIONS

21. Study the five kinds of critics. After you have seen a performance of a play of your choice, choose two or three of the critical approaches and write a short review from the standpoint of that critic.

22. Attend a performance and look for the assessment of that performance in a newspaper or journal. Then, compare/contrast that assessment with a scholarly article on the play. How do the kinds of writing differ?

23. Samuel Johnson wrote many prefaces to Shakespeare's plays. Choose a preface and analyze it. Is it scholarly? Is it dramatic criticism? How would you place it within the kinds of dramatic criticism? Rewrite it, using your imagination, to convert it into a contemporary review for a newspaper.

Chapter 7 (Brief only)
The Theatre of Our Times

1. Modern theatre marks its origin from
   a. 1875, with roots that developed out of eighteenth-century Enlightenment.
   b. 1776 and the rise of democracies and the birth of nation-states.
   c. 1865, the end of the Civil War, which marked the flourishing of civil liberties.
   d. 1616, the death of Shakespeare, after which theatre, with the concomitant Puritan closing of the theatres, would never recover.
   177

2. Among the intellectual revolutions that mark the birth of the modern theatre, which of the following do NOT apply?
   a. The revelations of Albert Einstein, Werner Heisenberg, and others removed all our "hitching posts in space" and established the human animal as little more than a transformation of kinetic energy.
   b. The biological theories of Charles Darwin made us understand that the human being is not a demigod and is linked to primal apes and prehistoric orangutans.
   c. The anthropologist Ruth Benedict argued that our laws are not handed to humanity from a single source but represent a range of traditions, wholly relative to the culture and climes we inhabit.
   * d. The writings of Claudius Ptolemy argue that humanity is a creature divinely created and that all human institutions, the theatre among them, are among divine and godly creations.
   179

3. According to Darwin, human beings can be understood as
   a. beings with an innate dignity and soul.
   * b. primates driven by the same biological urges as other animals.
   c. animals with reason who seek to understand their place in history.
   d. demigods with a divine origin.
   179

4. According to Sigmund Freud, human behavior is strongly influenced by
   a. the ability to reason.
   b. economic motivation and drive for success.
   * c. the Unconscious, with its infantile urges and suppressed fears and rages.
   d. class struggle.
   179

5. According to Karl Marx, human social behavior is motivated by
   a. the promptings of the unconscious.
   b. the desire to succeed at competition for food.
   c. a humanitarian impulse to share.
   * d. economic greed, class struggle, and primal amorality.
   179

148

6. Deliberately intending to free dramaturgy from formulas based on neoclassical constraint by means of flamboyant verse, boisterous action, epic adventure, passionate feeling, and sprawling dramatic structure, which artistic movement began in Europe in the late eighteenth century and reached its high point in the nineteenth century with such works as Goethe's *Faust?*
   a. Restoration
   b. Enlightenment
   c. Baroque
   * d. romanticism
   179

7. What did romanticism have in common with modernism?
   a. emphasis on rules of art
   * b. emphasis on nonconformity and individuality
   c. emphasis on reason and order
   d. emphasis on social virtues and proper/ethical human behavior
   180

8. Realistic theatre is conceived as
   * a. a laboratory where the nature of relationships, the ills of society, or the symptoms of a dysfunctional family are set down for the final judgment of impartial observers.
   b. a drawing room where the manners, costumes, and habits of a privileged class reflect the world of the audience.
   c. a court or public place where authority is pitted against adversaries of equal stature in a battle of cosmic proportion.
   d. an expression of a dream or irrational state where emotions and mood dominate plot and conflict.
   180

9. "The theatre of the fourth wall" refers to the central convention of realism, which is
   * a. the stage is conceived to be the same as life in a real-world setting, except that in the case of the stage one wall—the proscenium opening—has been removed.
   b. the human animal is seen to be like a rat in a maze, a creature bound by the strictures of walls, those walls being society, family, and economics.
   c. that "the fourth wall" refers to the mind and the ability of the imagination to create a frame around the experience and thus complete an experience just as a fourth wall completes a room.
   d. that the four walls refer to Marxist economics, Darwinian biological determinism, Freudian psychological determinism, and postmodern relativism.
   180

10. The founding playwright of the realist era and author of *Ghosts,* a play that ruthlessly explored the fullest implications of a hypocritical Victorian marriage, was
   * a. Henrik Ibsen.
   b. August Strindberg.
   c. Mario Tinburgen.
   d. Anton Chekhov.
   181

11. The plays of Ibsen treated
    a. the role of democracy in the communist world.
    * b. women's roles in society, hereditary disease, mercy killing, and political hypocrisy.
    c. environmental and animal rights.
    d. the conflict with economics and authoritarianism in establishing a new world order.
    182

12. "Problem play" refers to
    a. a play that violates the unities of the neoclassical aesthetic.
    * b. a realistic play that deals, narrowly, with a specific social problem.
    c. a play that portrays good and evil in strictly delimited ways to prevent moral ambiguity from creating a perceptual problem.
    d. a play that is difficult to produce because it calls for elaborate staging and machinery in order to create fires, automobile accidents, and airplane wrecks.
    182

13. Which of the following is NOT a realist dramatist correctly paired with his play?
    a. George Bernard Shaw, *Mrs. Warren's Profession*
    b. Gerhart Hauptmann, *The Weavers*
    c. Eugène Brieux, *Damaged Goods*
    * d. Antonin Artaud, *Jet of Blood*
    182

14. A physician by training and a writer by vocation, which playwright worked near the end of his career in association with Konstantin Stanislavski in the Moscow Theatre and was famous for *Uncle Vanya, The Seagull, The Cherry Orchard,* and *Three Sisters?*
    a. Alan Ayckbourne
    * b. Anton Chekhov
    c. August Strindberg
    d. Emile Pavrotti
    183

15. The stylistic apogee of realism was reached by
    * a. Anton Chekhov.
    b. August Strindberg.
    c. Henrik Ibsen.
    d. George Bernard Shaw.
    183

16. How did the naturalist theatre view humanity?
    a. Man was descended from Adam and Eve.
    * b. Man was merely a biological phenomenon whose behavior was determined entirely by genetic and social circumstances.
    c. Man was a creature existentially confused, trying to achieve identity through the recovery of a lost history.
    d. Man was a creature raised to mythical or god-like stature through the faculty of imagination.
    184

17. What was the subject matter of the naturalist theatre?
a. well-defined social issues like women's rights, venereal diseases, and inheritance laws
* b. a slice of life in which the characters were the play's entire subject, to which any topical issues were subsumed
c. conflicts with authority and tyrants
d. environmental and animal rights
184

• 18. Which theatre, exemplified by Sam Shepard's *Buried Child,* is ostensibly realistic but is actually suffused with menacing obscurity and mythic symbolism, steadily seeking out patterns beneath everyday surfaces and meanings in the silences that punctuate ordinary conversation?
a. naturalism
b. symbolism
* c. suprarealism
d. antirealism
184

 19. The symbolist theatre represented
* a. the inner realities that cannot be directly or literally perceived; thus characters represented philosophical ideals or warring internal forces in the human (or the artist's) soul.
b. human life as ordinary men and women might see it; thus characters represented emblems of the human condition.
c. the animal urges that motivate human action; thus characters represented instincts and passions.
d. the realities of social life in a driven, overbearing economic hardship; characters thus symbolized different classes.
188

20. Who inaugurated the symbolist theatre, begun in 1890 with an attack against the naturalist Théâtre Libre of André Antoine?
a. Franco Marinetti
b. Salvador Dali
* c. Paul Fort
d. Ernst Cassirer
188

21. Which of the following presented premieres by August Strindberg, Émile Zola, and Henrik Ibsen and went to great lengths to create realistic scenery?
a. Paul Fort
b. Arthur Rimbaud
* c. André Antoine
d. Paul Verlaine
188

22. Which of the following staged the poems and poetic plays of such writers as Arthur Rimbaud, Paul Verlaine, and Edgar Allen Poe and prevailed upon the leading impressionists to dress his stylized stage?
    a. Konstantin Stanislavski
    b. Antonin Artaud
    c. André Antoine
*   d. Paul Fort
    188

23. Which of the following naturalistic/realistic writers did NOT become symbolists?
    a. Henrik Ibsen
    b. George Bernard Shaw
    c. August Strindberg
*   d. Gordon Craig
    189

24. An experimental style of acting, characterized by expressive physical action and bold gesticulation, developed by the Russian constructivist Vsevolod Meyerhold in the 1920s in contrast to the style of Stanislavski, was called
    a. suprarealistic
    b. naturalistic
*   c. biomechanical
    d. impressionistic
    190

25. Which theatre wields reality in unexpected ways and freely enhances it with symbol and metaphor; strives to elucidate by parable and allegory; deconstructs and reconstructs by language, scenery, and lighting; makes explicit use of theatre's theatricality; and reaches for stylization, treating problems of psychology as problems of philosophy?
    a. symbolist theatre
    b. realist theatre
*   c. antirealist theatre
    d. neoclassical theatre
    192

26. Stylization is based on
    a. particulars.
*   b. patterns.
    c. concepts.
    d. incongruity.
    192

27. "Avant-garde," a military term literally meaning the vanguard or shock troops that initiate a major assault, was applied to
   a. the Italian aesthetics that promulgated communism through pamphlets.
   * b. the wave of playwrights and directors who openly assaulted realism in the first four decades of this century.
   c. postmodern painters.
   d. the wave of directors and performance artists who emerged in New York and Paris during the 1920s.
   193

28. Which Parisian play had the most violent opening in theatre history, such that the audience shouted, hissed, threw things, and shook their fists at the stage?
   * a. Jarry's *Ubu Roi*
   b. Brecht's *Mother Courage*
   c. Artaud's *Conquest of Mexico*
   d. Shepard's *Buried Child*
   193

29. Jarry's *Ubu Roi* was scandalous because
   a. it presented violations of propriety in subject matter for the first time.
   * b. it challenged conventions of decorous language.
   c. it was staged in a way that was shocking.
   d. the lead actor was notorious as a treasonous defector.
   193

30. What is "*le mot d'Ubu*"?
   a. *doit*
   * b. *merdre*
   c. *zut alors*
   d. *alouette*
   193

31. Exemplified by Eugene O'Neill's *The Hairy Ape,* which type of drama, in vogue in Germany during the first decades of the century, featured shocking dialogue, boldly exaggerated scenery, piercing sounds, bright lights, an abundance of primary colors, a not-very-subtle use of symbols, and a structure of short, stark, jabbing scenes building to a powerful or deafening climax?
   a. impressionism
   b. theater of cruelty
   * c. expressionism
   d. Dada
   195

32. In *Six Characters in Search of an Author,* Pirandello uses the theme of the theatricality of life and the life of theatricality to show
   * a. that everyday life is beset by the eternal confusion between appearance and reality.
   b. that appearances, while deceiving, can be grounded in an ultimate reality.
   c. the ultimate authority of truth to establish the difference between appearance and reality.
   d. that appearance is ephemeral and easy to dismiss.
   198

33. Which kind of theatre was developed by the French theorist Antonin Artaud (1896–1948), whose goal was to employ language more for its sound than for its meaning and to create a shocking stream of sensations rather than a coherent plot and cast of characters?
   a. theatre of the absurd
   b. epic theatre
 * c. theatre of cruelty
   d. absurdist theatre
   200

34. Which theatre would provide the "spectator with the true source of his dreams, in which his taste for crime, his erotic obsessions, his savagery, his illusions, his utopian ideals, even his cannibalism would surge forth"?
   a. theatre of the absurd
   b. epic theatre
 * c. theatre of cruelty
   d. theatre of blood
   200

35. What was the outcome of Artaud's venture in the theatre?
   a. His performances were box-office successes but literary failures.
   b. He enjoyed royal patronage and commercial success not seen since Molière.
 * c. His productions were failures, he was "expelled" from the surrealist movement, and he spent his later life abroad in mental institutions.
   d. Artaud's plays, never reaching the boards of any kind of theatre proper, were played in the streets and the lobbies of public buildings to antagonize politicians and critics.
   201

36. Which theatre includes plays that are derived from the philosophy found in the writings of Albert Camus, who likened the human condition to that of the mythological king Sisyphus, therefore symbolizing the search for meaning as an eternally futile task?
   a. theatre of cruelty
   b. epic theatre
 * c. theatre of the absurd
   d. theatre of alienation
   202

37. The philosophy that every individual seeks affirmation and self-realization in the eyes of the Other but can't find certification of final personal worth is consistent with
   a. Strindberg's view of expressionism.
   b. the role of the unconscious in Ibsen.
 * c. Sartre's existentialism.
   d. Dali's surrealism.
   202

38. Which of the following is true of characterization in Sartre's *No Exit?*
   * a. The characters represent philosophical conditions rather than psychological wholes.
   b. The characters represent the essential bifurcation of the human condition into appearance and reality.
   c. The characters represent psychologically unified beings rather than types.
   d. The characters represent the role of the unconscious when it is forced into action in social situations.
   202

39. Written by a well-known French existentialist, which play shows hell to be a room without windows or mirrors where ill-matched characters confront an infinite bleakness, so that hell is other people?
   a. Artaud's *Jet of Blood*
   b. Pirandello's *Six Characters in Search of an Author*
   * c. Sartre's *No Exit*
   d. Shaw's *Major Barbara*
   202

40. Which playwright, born in Dublin in 1906, had a career marked by artistic vagabondage, during which time he wrote several short stories and poems, among which *Waiting for Godot* stands as his masterpiece?
   a. James Joyce
   * b. Samuel Beckett
   c. Eugene O'Neill
   d. John Millington Synge
   204

41. In which play does a good-hearted prostitute receive a gift of money from three itinerant gods and use the money to start a tobacco business?
   a. Shaw's *Man and Superman*
   b. O'Neill's *Mourning Becomes Electra*
   * c. Brecht's *Good Woman of Sezuan*
   d. Beckett's *Happy Days*
   207

42. Which theatre attempted to alienate the audience by repudiating realistic conventions through a didactic performance style, an acting style that required the actor to "demonstrate" rather than integrate with his character, and a stage that called attention to its own artificiality?
   * a. Brecht's theater of alienation
   b. Artaud's theater of cruelty
   c. Pirandello's theatricalism
   d. Beckett's realism
   207

43. Who is the foremost writer of light comedy for the stage in America?
  a. Paul Simon
  b. Alan Ayckbourne
  c. Sam Shepard
* d. Neil Simon
  209

44. In which play do the characters consist of four couples who find themselves in one bedroom after another, by turns, in a play that builds on animated verbal exchanges, comic business, and pratfalls?
  a. Neil Simon's *Room with a View*
* b. Alan Ayckbourne's *Bedroom Farce*
  c. Terence Plautus's *Confusions*
  d. Stephen Sondheim's *Not Again*
  209

45. Which play is a dramatic case study, i.e., a play that dramatizes the situation of a character's distress and furnishes a perspective for the playwright's philosophical investigations?
* a. Arthur Kopit's *Wings*
  b. Sam Shepard's *Fool for Love*
  c. Alan Ayckbourne's *Bedroom Farce*
  d. Stephen Sondheim's *Assassins*
  212

46. Which political satire, written in a racy rhyming verse, explores the vagaries of arbitrage stock trading on the London and international markets?
  a. Arthur Kopit's *Wings*
  b. Sam Shepard's *Fool for Love*
  c. Alan Ayckbourne's *Bedroom Farce*
* d. Caryl Churchill's *Serious Money*
  215

47. Based on a contemporary British version by author Christopher Bond, which play tells the story of the "Demon Barber of Fleet Street," who decides to wreak revenge upon a corrupt English judiciary by baking their ground-up corpses into meat pies?
  a. *Wings*
* b. *Sweeney Todd*
  c. *Buried Child*
  d. *Jet of Blood*
  216

48. What is the name given to the Japanese puppet theatre?
  a. Kabuki
  b. Nō
* c. Bunraku
  d. Kyōgen
  218

49. Which of the following is NOT true of Asiatic theatre?
    a. Language in Asian theatre is invariably rhythmic and melodic and is appreciated for its sound as much as (or more than) for its meaning.
    b. The metaphysical roots of Asian theatre lie in the timeless meditation on human existence that is at the heart of Indian Hindu and Buddhist cultures.
    c. Asian theatre is heavily stylized, largely a matter of formalized performances.
*   d. Asian theatre is like early Greek drama, emphasizing plotting and dramaturgical cohesiveness.
    218–219

50. What is the name given to the sylized movement in Kabuki drama in which one or more actors move with rapidly increasing violence until they suddenly freeze in a contorted position that they hold for several seconds?
*   a. *mie*
    b. *onnagata*
    c. *hikinuki*
    d. *koken*
    224

ESSAY QUESTIONS

51. Discuss "the buried child" in Sam Shepard's *Buried Child* for its literal and symbolic meanings.

52. Playwrights such as Ibsen, Strindberg, Hauptmann, and Shaw came to straddle the naturalist and symbolist movements. Take one of the works of any of these playwrights, and analyze the naturalist/symbolist elements.

53. Compare and contrast Ibsen's *Ghosts* with Strindberg's *Ghost Sonata*. What do the plays have in common? How do ghosts function in each of these plays? How are these plays different?

54. The confrontation between realist and symbolist theatres informed every aspect of theatre production. Discuss how this confrontation was played out in acting style or stage design.

55. Argue for or against: In Alfred Jarry's *Ubu Roi,* there is no poetic justice. Then use your response as the basis to speculate on the relationship between a play's form and the audience's sense of ethics. Does aesthetic justice persuade us that there is also social justice?

56. Discuss how O'Neill, in *The Hairy Ape,* uses the set—the sounds, colors, space—to parallel Yank's feelings. Is Yank bound by his surroundings, or do these surroundings offer the milieu in which he is most alive?

57. Consider Pirandello's play, *Six Characters in Search of an Author,* as offering a statement about human identity. Write an essay in which you explain how all the characters add up to offer a view of identity.

58. Choose a play from any collection, or consult with your teacher in your selection. From that play, select a scene and explain how you would stage it in the spirit of the theatre of cruelty.